How
Modern
Should
Theology Be?

By HELMUT THIELICKE

Translated by H. GEORGE ANDERSON

FORTRESS PRESS   Philadelphia

This book is a translation of *Wie Modern Darf die Theologie Sein?*
Vier Modelle heutiger Verkündigung,
copyright © 1967 by Quell Verlag, Stuttgart, Germany.

Scripture quotations from the Revised
Standard Version of the Bible,
copyrighted 1946 and 1952 by the
Division of Christian Education of the
National Council of the Churches
of Christ in the United States of America,
are used by permission.

Library of Congress Catalog Card Number 69-14620

484J69   Printed in the U.S.A.   1-287

Stand by us, Lord, for night is coming
        and the day is drawing to a close.
Stand by us, and by your whole church.
Stand by us in the twilight of the day,
        in the twilight of life,
        and in the twilight of the world.
Stand by us with your grace and goodness,
        with your holy Word and Sacrament,
        and with your comfort and blessing.
Stand by us when we are overtaken by
        the night of trouble and anxiety,
        the night of doubt and despair,
        and the night of bitter death.
Stand by us, and by all your faithful ones
        now and forever.

                —Saturday evening prayer in
                    St. Michael's Church, Hamburg

Contents

To the Reader

The chapters which follow were first preached as sermons at Saturday afternoon worship services. They are addressed to people who have been reading in newspapers and magazines about the controversy now going on among theologians. I wanted to give some perspective to the questions presently under debate, and also to show their significance for our faith. Consequently, I am addressing myself not just to people whose roots are in the Christian tradition, but to all people who have questions, people who are looking for something. Naturally I do not assume any specialized knowledge on the part of the reader. I expect only a certain open-mindedness, and a readiness to concentrate a little on following a train of thought.

I have selected four themes that are central to the current debate, and related each of them to a particular "text" of Scripture which is then expounded. In addition, I have set down yet another passage called a "reading." The readings, which originally formed a part of the opening worship, have some special significance for the topics under discussion; either they shed light on the subject from another angle, or they are referred to in the discourses themselves. In making them available here for consultation I have used my own translation, which attempts to express accurately the sense of the original. I did not deliberately set out to make the biblical passages sound "modern." It just happened to turn out that way—to my own surprise.

How
Modern
Should
Theology Be?

READING

When he was in Athens, Paul grew angry as he saw the city's idolatry. He argued with the Jews and other devout people in the synagogue and also with anyone he met in the market place. It was in this way that some philosophically-minded people—Epicureans and Stoics—got into a dispute with him. Things were said like, "Is this nut putting us on?" and, "It sounds like he's trying to get something across about foreign religions." That was because Paul had preached about Jesus and his resurrection. Finally they pulled him aside to the Aeropagus and said to him, "Would you kindly let us in on this new teaching that you represent? We have never heard things like that before."

Now it is important to know that the foreigners there, as well as the Athenians, liked nothing better than hearing and telling the newest and latest thing.

Then Paul stepped to the center of the Aeropagus and began his speech: "Wherever I look I discover how religious you are. As I walked through the city, observing your places of worship, my eye ˜fell upon an altar that bore the inscription: "To an unknown god." Thus you honor a power which you do not know, and *even though* you do not know it. And now I am the one to proclaim that power to you and to tell you who this unknown god is."   Acts 17:16–23

HOW MODERN SHOULD THEOLOGY BE?

TEXT

The important thing for the Jews is that God makes himself known by miraculous signs, while the Greeks look for the "God of the philosophers." But we preach the crucified Christ, and this picture of divine weakness scandalizes the Jews, while the Greeks see it as the exact opposite of philosophical reason—they see it as nonsense. But in Christ those who have answered God's call —whether Jews or Greeks—encounter the power of God rather than his weakness, his wisdom rather than his folly.

Although through Christ I myself have now become free of all human bondage, I have made myself the servant of all men simply to win over as many as possible.

Thus, I have become like a Jew to the Jews so that I could reach them effectively. As far as I myself am concerned, my faith has freed me from the Law. But when I am dealing with legalists who are still bound to the Mosaic Law, I put myself in their shoes in order to reach them.

On the other hand, when I meet the Greeks and those who do not have the Law of Moses, I go back to being like one of them. Yet I am personally always "under God" and therefore by no means "uncommitted." Christ, of course, is the standard to which I am bound. Yet I operate on the level of the lawless in order to reach them.

In short, I have become all things to all men so that, in one way or another, I can save some. To the weak I became weak— they too were a concern of mine. I do it all for the gospel's sake, identifying with everyone in its behalf.

I Cor. 1:22–25; 9:19–23

How modern should theology be? Isn't that a strange and somewhat untimely question? Who would ever think of asking how modern a car should be, or a dictating machine or laboratory equipment? People would think that anyone who asked such questions was probably a little touched or an oddball. It is obvious

2

that mechanical equipment can never be too modern. Modernization in this area simply means improvement, elimination of weak spots, smoother operation. Yesterday's best is not good enough for today.

But what about theology? Isn't the question of modernization out of place here? After all, the situation is different from that in industry. There are faithful servants of God who get chills up and down their spines when they hear the phrase "modern theology." And then there are people of our day—honest questioners and intellectuals of every sort—who find in the phrase a note of liberation and hope. It seems to promise one more chance for a faith that was just about on its last legs. Modern theology seems to offer a new lease on life. It seems to suggest that you can experience faith in Christ as something current and up-to-date. You don't have to pretend that you're living in a bygone era.

This word "modern," then, although it is the trademark of quality in industry, triggers a wild verbal battle on the field of theology. Newspapers and magazines, alert to what "grabs" people, open their columns to this sort of agitation. At a gathering in West Germany in 1966 twenty thousand people declared modern theology to be the sheep's clothing in which the "ancient foe" was currently camouflaging himself. One side shouts "Spirit of God" and the other shouts "Beelzebub"—the battle cries seem to be diametrically opposed.

What are we to make of all this? We certainly cannot remain neutral in the conflict when we see how the most precious possession entrusted to us—our faith—

3

is wrenched this way and that. One person says that modern theology makes faith possible again for twentieth-century man. Another takes the opposite position and claims that modern theology saps, denies, and destroys faith.

Anyone interested in the history of words will soon discover that the word "modern" has long been a storm center in theology. It first turned up over seven hundred years ago as a term of abuse applied to those who wanted to modify tried and true traditions through various innovations. But the people lampooned as "modern" were quick to hurl the insult right back by calling the conservative defenders of tradition "reactionaries," petrified monuments of a long-dead cause.

In this chapter and those that follow I should like to clarify the issues a little if I can by setting down a few preliminary observations which we will then want to think through—without, of course, exhausting the question.

Ortega y Gasset once said that to be modern is to have a sense of standing at the pinnacle of history and from that vantage point looking down on all that went before. Taking it from there, the Christian might ask himself if his faith and the way it has been formulated is modern in this sense. There are reasons for thinking this may not be the case.

The basic truths of the faith are obviously constant and unalterable. That God is the creator of heaven and earth, that man has eaten the forbidden fruit, that he is a sinner enslaved to the futility of all that passes away, and that despite all this God has remained

4

faithful to him, seeking him through pain, and that Jesus Christ is the seal of this faithfulness—all these truths are obviously of a supertemporal validity. They were well known to our fathers, and hopefully will still be well known to our grandchildren. We said that, in industry, to modernize means to surpass and improve. But how are *these* truths to be surpassed or improved upon? If it is true that in and of himself man is lost and in need of salvation, then it is always true and can never be made any truer. Whoever attempts to modernize something about that fact is bound to be suspected of wanting to change it, or of falsifying it by trying to squeeze it into more stylish and palatable forms.

And isn't it true that symptoms of this sort do seem to appear in what today is called—somewhat unfortunately—modern theology? Doesn't present-day theology seem to be tearing down everything that "people at the pinnacle of history" think irritating, obsolete, or out of step with the last word in science (whatever that is!)? The miracle stories are lopped off in the name of nature's conservation of energy. Transcendent interventions and acts of God may no longer occur, because an event without a natural cause contradicts all the axioms underlying our current picture of the world. But doesn't that also do away with the resurrection of Christ and his coming again at the end of time?

Granted, so-called modern theology does not mean to expunge all that from the church's confession of faith. There is hardly anyone, even among the most extreme radicals, who wishes to throw the Apostles' Creed out the window. Even they continue to say the words "born of the Virgin Mary . . . rose again . . . ascended into heaven." But all this is no longer considered a statement of facts, for these facts are supposed to have no place in the tightly-knit fabric of earthly events inasmuch as they cannot be reconciled with the premises governing our scientific and technological mastery of the world. They are no longer understood as facts, but merely as symbols, deeply meaningful truths of existence expressed in the language of legend and myth. Therefore our job is to decode this language, reverently and respectfully drawing out its hidden truths for our generation.

Now the people who take this position are also devout. They too want to keep the faith. They too have been touched by the truths contained in that remarkable old Book and do not want to abandon them. I say this to their credit—even though I myself do not see eye to eye with them—and in so doing I probably step on the toes of many of the so-called faithful who regard modern theology as a snare and a delusion, and its advocates as demonic rascals. I wager that some of these "faithful" folk may be further discomfited on the Day of Judgment because of the idle words and often false witness they have spoken against neighbors holding divergent views. Such pious protests frequently do not stem from faith, but from the kind of lazy thinking and weakness of faith that bars the door to further inquiry.

Yet the question remains: Haven't the so-called modern theologians really given up a decisive point when they appear to make mere parables out of God's demonstrations of power, when they tailor the ancient truths to fit our current thought patterns? At any rate that is the question that alarms many pious folk—and often, one must admit, with good reason.

Nevertheless, we must be careful. The situation is not that simple. The truths of yesterday will certainly still be true today and tomorrow. The question is whether they can always be *expressed* in the same way. The Pythagorean theorem, for example, will undoubtedly remain valid for every age; an astronaut orbiting the moon can hardly formulate it differently from the way Copernicus or Galileo did long ago. But does the same principle of continuity apply with respect to expressions of the truth about God and man? Does it apply to the affirmations of Christian faith?

There is a very strong indication that the situation in this respect is very different indeed. I refer to the simple fact that there is such a thing as preaching. Why don't we content ourselves merely with reading Bible passages aloud and reciting the Apostles' Creed? After all, there we have all Christian truth contained in its original form and boiled down to the barest essentials. Why do we have to have long sermons *about* these things instead of simply reading them in their classic originals? And what effort we expend every day—especially on Sundays—in stating the old in ever new ways! It's like diluting good strong soup with water! Why all this watered-down rhetoric, this hemming and hawing, instead of letting the word of God ring forth the way it was written?

7

The way it was written? What would that mean? If I were to read the Bible to you in its original Hebrew and Greek, hardly anyone would understand it. At the very least it must be translated. But what does it mean to translate? It obviously means that I must take the old story and put it into the language of today. And this must be done repeatedly; even the best known translations of the Bible have many parts that are no longer understandable. But translating means more than a mere recasting in words. It means making "relevant" too, so that the hearer remarks, "Why that has to do with me!"

It's terrifying to think that I could stand here and preach about things that are more important than food or drink—I could speak about whether we are missing the very point of life and dooming ourselves to meaninglessness or whether we can triumph over trouble and guilt—and all the while there could be someone sitting there on the left aisle, seven rows back, stretching himself in boredom and thinking, "That's not my cup of tea. It has nothing to do with me. The only thing that concerns me is how I can earn more, work less, and get the most fun out of indulging my drives and passions." If I have been given the task of setting forth the ultimate questions of existence and yet am unsuccessful in showing that these questions are even a matter of *concern*—that for each of us they are a matter of life and death—then either I have botched the whole job, or God has condemned us in this hour to hardness of heart.

It is the very purpose of the gospel, though, to be of vital concern to man. When a prisoner on death row is told that he has been freed, so that his life, instead of ending grimly, is just beginning again, he is quite naturally concerned in a basic way. His whole life hangs in the balance, concentrated, one might say, in this single moment. It would be ridiculous to suppose that he would doze off at such a time, bored and uninvolved. Well, this is precisely the way in which the gospel concerns men also. Here too we lose our chains, and the things that formerly tyrannized us—worry about tomorrow, the burden of unforgiven sin, the hate that ties our heart in knots, anxiety that conjures up ghostly fears—all are suddenly robbed of their power. They may no longer lead us to our doom.

It's remarkable, isn't it, that while this little story about the prisoner who is so deeply concerned with his sudden reprieve sets forth a truth so obvious as to border on banality, the acquittal from God which the gospel brings just leaves us cold. It doesn't concern us at all. For if it were taken seriously, whether the news of acquittal was believed or not, it would really be hot copy. People might doubt it, but they would discuss it! For it would be at least as newsworthy as the threat of atomic war or a presidential heart attack.

Why is it then, that time after time the gospel does not stimulate that type of reaction? Why is it often laid away in the drawers of memory as an irrelevent truth we once learned by rote as children? Or, to put the question in a positive form, what *is* of concern to us, anyway?

In general, the only things in life that excite me—or even interest me—are those matters that concern my own existence. For example, if I am a typical bookworm who buries himself in old tomes and hardly ever sticks his nose outside the library, then I just won't be interested in someone telling me about the fine points of fly casting. On the other hand, an exposition of Kant's *Critique of Pure Reason* would be all Greek to someone who is completely immersed in the outdoor life. For those who understand Kant, his work is tremendously interesting, just as fly casting is terribly exciting to the fanatical angler. But neither of these areas mean a thing to people for whom the questions of philosophy or the adventures of fishing are irrelevant.

Once we are clear on this basically simple set of circumstances, we suddenly understand how they apply to the gospel. As long as I can discover no connection between the gospel and the problems of my life, then it has nothing to say to me and I am not interested. And that is precisely why the gospel must be preached afresh and told in new ways to every generation, since every generation has its own unique questions. This is why the gospel must constantly be forwarded to a new address, because the recipient is repeatedly changing his place of residence. The God of the Law, the Last Judgment, and hell were real in Luther's day, and he applied himself with single-minded fervor to the question of how he could survive the trial and come off justified. A man like that, naturally, lived in an entirely different frame of reference from a contemporary of ours who, like Camus, believes in the absurdity of life and concludes—sadly or cynically—that "God is dead." If I preach to this modern man on how he can avoid the Last Judgment and find a gracious God, he will just shake his head. That is simply not his problem. How can anyone who thinks God doesn't even exist be interested in finding out how to gain the grace of this non-existent God?

In short, if the basic questions of life have shifted, then I must redirect the message of the gospel. Otherwise I am answering questions that have never even been asked. And upon hearing such answers, my opposite number will just shake his head and say, "That's no concern of mine. It has nothing to do with me."

This is why theology can never be modern enough. For when the gospel tells a man that God is good to him, that God has not given up on him—no matter how far he strays or to what pig-trough he descends—that message must be delivered in ever new and constantly modernized ways. The far countries and the pig-troughs, the forms of guilt and anxiety, are constantly changing, even though they are ultimately only variations on one and the same alienation from God. Take a modern man like Gottfried Benn. He hears the trumpets of nothingness blowing on the edge of life and feels naked meaninglessness clutching at him, without the comfort of knowing that Someone has "higher thoughts" about him. The message of Jesus will reach such a man from other directions and with other overtones than it would come to a medieval man who took for granted that God's arms embraced the universe, and whose only question was whether those hands would beckon in love or threaten to discipline him.

To me, the greatest miracle of the gospel has always been that it includes *all* these human possibilities and seeks out everyone in his own individual "far country." It knows how to find the prostitute in her pitiful degradation and the rich young man in his glittering poverty. It addresses both the opportunistic Pontius Pilate and the despairing Canaanite woman. It reaches a Luther wrestling with his conscience, and it wrings one last hope of peace from the unhappy Rufus who, in James Baldwin's *Another Country,* plunges to his death with a curse on his lips. They are all held safely within the gospel, embraced by it. Their addresses are all written on the great all-inclusive envelope. Christ himself is there for all of them, and also for those dead ones who mourn the "death of God," who groan under—or even flirt with—the absurdity of existence and who cry out with Jean Paul's dead Christ, "O Father, O Father, where is thine infinite bosom, that I may be at rest?"*

That is how the old melody of the gospel must be transposed into ever new tonalities—not only modern ones, but even "atonal" ones. And that is precisely what Paul meant in the words of the text. The Greeks asked about what held the world together at its inmost core; they were interested in speculating about the foundations of the universe. Therefore Paul goes into this question in order to "involve" the Greeks. Granted, he does not do it—as later apologists did—simply to

---

* Jean Paul Friedrich Richter, *Flower, Fruit, and Thorn Pieces or The Married Life, Death, and Wedding of the Advocate of the Poor, Firmian Stanislaus Siebenkäs,* First Flower-Piece, trans. Edward Henry Noel (Boston: Tickner and Fields, 1863), I, 352.

plug for Christ as an answer to their philosophical questions. Rather he does it in such a way that he crosses out their questions, so to speak, and makes them see that God is *not* to be found in the speculative stratosphere. They should look in exactly the opposite direction—in the depth of human misery and utter abandonment, on a criminal's cross. This is where Christ's love drove him, and only those who seek him in this ungodly wretchedness will find him. Only those who take up Jesus' cross grasp his hand. All others end up with Pascal's "God of the philosophers"—an idea—which is just another name for a dumb idol.

And although Paul thus becomes a Greek to the Greeks, meeting them—and also arguing with them—on their own intellectual level, he immediately shifts his tactics when dealing with Jews. He tells them the same thing he said to the Greeks, but he says it in a quite different way. The Jews wrestled with the Law of God. They worked his commandments out to the nth degree and developed an immensely complicated code of behavior. The result was either that they entangled themselves in the hopeless jumble of these demands and despaired of ever becoming righteous, or—and this is just as bad—they fell prey to the illusion that they could fulfill everything and became pharisaically self-righteous. In this situation Paul lets the gospel take hold in a quite different way, so that self-righteousness and despair are no longer the only alternatives. He shows the Jews that *another* has fulfilled for us what no man can fulfill by himself, and that we are now free, mature sons of God. We do not have to win God's favor, he tells them, it is already given to us. This is the gospel as stated for the Jews.

Thus Paul is the perfect example of what one could call, in a good sense, a modern theologian. He constantly redirects his message, adapting himself to the person he is addressing at the moment. And what Paul did then, we must do today. In the Pauline sense we must become a Marxist to the Marxists, an existentialist to the existentialists, and perhaps a hippie to the hippies. Of course we must first love them too, and then in love find out *why* they are what they are. Only in that way will we discover the particular gospel addressed to them.

But wait a minute. What does this mean? Does it imply that we should accommodate ourselves and simply ape the people we would reach? Far from it! Paul actually contradicted the Greeks and Jews and showed them that God was completely different from what they had expected. But it was in terms of *their* suppositions and notions that he searched them out. He met their questions on their level. That makes all the difference. He did not ape what they were saying just to make the gospel palatable. The great biblical theologian Martin Kähler has formulated this decisive difference more profoundly and precisely than anyone else: "Paul indeed stated that he wanted to be a Jew to the Jews and a Greek to the Greeks, but he refused to be a miracle-worker among the Jews or a cultural messiah among the Greeks."

Somewhere in this area may be the Achilles' heel of what we today call modern theology. Of course I hesitate to mention it because it gets us into questions that are

14

not easily treated in a sermon. If, on the one hand, I say that theology can never be too modern since it must constantly be addressed and readdressed to contemporaries, then, on the other hand, it is also true that the whole effort amounts to nothing if modernity is made the criterion, becoming an end in itself. I can only point out the problem involved here and let it go at that.

On the one hand, the gospel must be put in modern terms. This is the only way modern man—including my neighbor—can assimilate it. Otherwise it will inevitably remain foreign to him—and in fact he must reject it— if he does not understand how it has anything to do with the problems he faces, or if it seems to be diametrically opposed to what his current view of truth holds to be possible. If the gospel were to demand that he also take over the ancient pre-Copernican picture of the universe as it is contained in that ancient book we call the Bible, then he would have to deny himself (literally!). I can really make the gospel my own only if I may believe it with my eyes open, only if my faith does not force me to throw out something, or ignore something, or forget it for a while.

Moreover, this is not merely a condition that I as a modern man have imposed on faith. Faith itself demands it. For Jesus Christ wants me totally. He wants me to belong to him with more than my conscience, my emotions, and my anxieties: he wants my reason, my knowledge, and all the areas of my consciousness as well. But if I have to repress and suppress anything that I as a scientist or historian know, if I run to meet him with a mind that is not awake and intact and able to say,

15

"Here you have me with all I am and have, including my knowledge and my reason," then I do not belong to him totally. At most I am placing at his disposal only a part of me—my religiosity or my pious feelings. Jesus Christ, though, wants all or nothing. The lukewarm and halfhearted, those who are merely curious about religion, who never can come to the point of giving themselves completely, are always the losers. Perhaps it would be better for them if they remained blind (John 9:41).

On the other hand, no matter how imperative it is for the Greek, the Jew, and modern man with their respective views of truth to make the gospel their own, it is just as important to remember that Paul never wanted to accommodate himself to the Jews and Greeks—the modern men of that day and this. Instead he met them on the level of their own life and thought precisely for the purpose of calling them into question.

Couldn't this be just the place where today we so frequently go astray? Granted, we want to be modern men to modern man. So far, so good. But couldn't it be that, from this point on, we get off the track? We are just as convinced as our contemporaries that the world is a self-contained energy system and that all life ends in death. Now it could be—and often is—that we make this contemporary world view absolute and glibly say that "if it's not possible, it can't happen." It is not possible for God to stay in control of the world and its laws; it is not possible for him to breach the line of death's decree at some point; it is not possible for him to appear "once" in the midst of our history as an "individual" (Kierkegaard) —therefore it cannot happen!

When we make this move, we have passed the point of no return. From here on, the modernity of our minds quickly leads us to fortify ourselves against the coming of God. We will welcome only the God who fulfills the conditions which we must impose in order to be able to accept him as God. We are ready to accept him as God if he does nothing more than merely clarify the meaning of our life or disclose the depth of our existence for us. But we won't have him if he is going to call all of our pet theories into question. We intend to remain Greeks and Jews—modern men—and God may as well get used to it! If he will allow that, then he is welcome —why not?—to be the essence of universal wisdom to us Greeks, the heavenly representative of righteousness to us Jews, and the key to the depth of existence for us existentialists.

When we think this way, modernity becomes a curse. For the addressee—the Jew or Greek—simply refuses receipt of the divine truth if the package in which it arrives doesn't suit him. Or else he opens it carefully and sets aside that portion of the contents which is unacceptable to him. To be modern in this very self-righteous, cocksure, and supercilious sense, is nothing less than a criminal attack on the truth of God. That is, we permit ourselves the privilege of deciding what can be truth for us. In reality the situation is quite the reverse: God's truth questions *us* much more than we question *it*. "Christianity," says Georges Bernanos, "has brought one truth into the world which nothing can ever stop, because it is prior to even the most unreflective conscience and because man immediately recognizes himself in it:

God has rescued every one of us, and each of us is worth the blood of God." We, however, put the question differently: "Are *you*, God, worthy of *us?* We think your truth will have to be worked over a little before it will suit our vital questions and our thinking habits!" This would indeed be the kind of a modern theology that delivers itself up to judgment, a judgment which curiously enough—yet quite logically—the theology itself could no longer recognize.

This sort of modern theology has always been with us. It is nothing new; it goes back two thousand years. Again and again the package of divine truth has been opened and everything which didn't suit was laid aside. Over and over, the figure of Jesus has been horribly amputated until he fit the Procrustean bed of what one particular age held to be "modern" concepts. In the first centuries he was shaped according to the Greek logos concept and made to square with philosophy. During the Enlightenment he was made into a rational being, under idealism an idea, in liberal protestantism a teacher of morality, and by the existentialists a Socrates who reveals the depths of human existence to us. Through the whole history of the church Jesus Christ has suffered a process of repeated crucifixion. He has been scourged and bruised and locked in the prison of countless systems and philosophies. Treated as a body of thought, he has literally been lowered into conceptual graves and covered with stone slabs so that he might not arise and trouble us any more. Hasn't this process rendered him harmless by enrolling him in the club of human thought? That is what Hölderlin tried to do when, with a despairing effort in one of his later hymns, "The Only One," he put Christ on Olympus and let him appear as one among many gods. Isn't the history of Christianity the sum of the fatal misunderstandings which have arisen over Jesus Christ? Isn't the history of the church to the present day one vast experiment gone awry, a dreadful victory of the currently "modern" over the Nazarene who must bear it all helplessly and silently?

This is a bold question—the boldest anyone can pose from the pulpit. Yet it is comforting to ask it. For even though the thought may overwhelm us for a moment with despair, that same moment makes us witnesses of a miracle. No mere *thought*, you see, could ever have survived such strong medicine. No human *idea* could have endured such attacks, amputations, and crucifixions without ending in the graveyard of intellectual history, where only the historian would still find anything worthwhile.

But this is the miracle, that from this succession of conceptual graves Jesus Christ has risen again and again! None of them became his last resting place. No tombstone was ever heavy enough to hold him. Again and again, wherever two or three are gathered in his name, he steps into their midst and is present with his strength and consolation. Again and again he appears at the deathbed and holds up the head of the sufferer in his final weakness. And men face death for him with songs of praise on their lips.

By the now-empty grave, however, the angel asks us also, "Why do you seek the living among the dead?

19

Your graves too could not hold him." The fact that we gather in his congregation, that we hear his word, speak with him and praise him—this is the great refutation of that horrible vision which sees men burying the living Lord in their conceptual graves and making him a harmless "historical figure."

Be comforted and unafraid, for I say to you now in his name: Jesus Christ himself is already far out in front of every age that attempts to come to grips with him. He sees to that. He is more up-to-date than any "modern" age which feels itself superior to all that has gone before. His promise still holds true for us. He is always the newest and most up-to-the-minute on this old-fashioned earth, the living one on the field of dead bones. For he said, "Behold I am with you always, even unto the end of the world."

How
Reliable
Are the Biblical
Accounts of Jesus?

READING

A man put on a big dinner party and invited many people. At meal-time he sent out his servant to tell those who were invited, "Now is the time to come; everything is ready."

But then one after another began to excuse himself.

The first said, "I have bought a field and I simply must get out and look at it. Be so kind as to consider me excused!"

Another sent back, "I have obtained a span of oxen and am on my way to inspect them. Please excuse me!"

And then another answered, "I have just gotten married; it is impossible for me to come!"

When the servant got back, he reported everything to his master. Upon hearing it, the man became very angry and ordered him, "Go, as quickly as you can, into the streets and alleys of the city and this time bring me the poor, the crippled, the blind, and the lame."

Then the servant informed him, "Master, your orders have been carried out, but there still is room for more."

So the master answered, "Then go out also to the highways and hedges and use a little pressure to get the people to come along, so that we'll have a full house. I tell you, none of those whom I originally invited will now eat my dinner."

Luke 14:16–24

HOW MODERN SHOULD THEOLOGY BE?

TEXT

Many people have already set out to report the events concerning Jesus which happened among us. They have followed what was handed down to us from the very men who were on the scene from the beginning as eyewitnesses and whom the Word then took into its service as witnesses.

For my part I have followed them step for step and point by point from the beginning on and have decided to write it down for you, honored Theophilus, exactly and in chronological order. I do it in order to demonstrate the reliability of the words by which you have been instructed.

Luke 1:1–4

First of all, *one* thing must be emphasized: I have handed on to you only that which I myself have received—that, in accordance with the witness of Scripture, Christ died for our sins, that he was buried and then arose on the third day—again in accordance with Scripture. Then he appeared to Cephas, and afterward to the Twelve. Later, over five hundred brothers at once were aware of his appearing. Most of them are still alive among us; only a few have died. Ultimately, he appeared to James and finally to all the apostles. In the end he appeared to me too, although I was as unready for it as a premature baby is for life.

But if it should not be true that Christ was raised like this, then our preaching would be sound and fury, and your faith would be rubbish.

If we pin our hope in Christ only on *this* life, then we are the most pitiful of all mankind.

I Cor. 15:3–8, 14, 19

These texts are monumental, aren't they? They exhibit a granite-like certainty about those things that happened concerning Jesus. It was still possible to interview eyewitnesses; the chain of tradition seemed without gaps.

How nice it would be if we today could be equally certain about these assurances. But can we? After all, the New Testament writers were men of a bygone day, and what was obvious to them is not nearly so plausible to us. Where they listened to a miracle story with a pious thrill, we are skeptical and go over it with a fine-toothed comb. We know—and are quick to point out—that the universe is a self-contained system. Therefore, it is not so easy for us to accept talk about transcendent interventions like heavenly choirs, stilling of storms, and raising the dead.

In addition, our historical methods have been gradually refined until they are infinitely more exact than they were in Luke's day. Luke's historical efforts would probably not be precise enough for a twentieth-century Theophilus. And certainly everyone who reads the newspapers and magazines today knows that what Luke thought to be absolutely certain is now open to question. Hasn't he so fantastically confused the historical and the legendary—what is reported and what is commentary—that the contours of the actual events concerning Jesus Christ have eroded away and the figure of the Lord himself has faded beyond recognition?

But why harp on such historical accounts and the question of their reliability anyway? Aren't there enough passages in the Gospels which are self-authenticating? Don't they have the ring of truth in themselves, so that they don't even need historical attestation? "Whatever you wish that men would do to you, do so to them" (Matt. 7:12). Certainly these words of Jesus are valid even without the authority of historicity; they would be valid even if the Lord had never said them. Am I wrong? Or how about the lilies of the field, blooming free of care as they teach us to trust in the source of all life. All of this packs an authority of its own; we detect the bedrock of truth in it.

If this is so, then why all this nosing around in history? Why the question about whether Jesus really said it or whether it was later attributed to him? Why ask if this or that really happened or was merely attributed to him at a later date? Doesn't this way of putting the question lead us into a blind alley? Did not Luke and Paul themselves stumble into the same blind alley when they made everything depend on witnesses, reports, and traditions?

Are we moderns really the first to see through this false quest for the historical? Were Paul and Luke really so naive? For myself, I am in favor of taking Paul and Luke seriously for once—maybe that makes me pretty naive—and pondering what they could have had in mind when they accentuated the factuality and reality of the events so unequivocally.

In his story of *The Plague at Bergamo* Jens Peter Jacobsen tells of a pale, young, and fanatic monk who preaches on how Christ was crucified while the boozing, brawling soldiers beneath his cross mocked him. Then, the story goes, the Son of God was filled to overflowing with anger and scorn. He realized that those clods there were not worthy of salvation. He tore free his feet and his hands over the heads of the nails, leaped down upon the earth, snatched up his garment—for which they were rolling dice—flung it round himself with the wrath of a king, and ascended into heaven. And the cross stood empty, and the great work of redemption was never fulfilled. "There is no mediator between God and us," cried the monk, "There is no Jesus who died for us on the cross. Do you hear? There is no Jesus who died for us on the cross!"*

Roger Caillois, too, has retold the gospel in similar terms in his novel about Pontius Pilate. Jesus of Nazareth is acquitted by Pilate and so does not go to the cross. He spends the rest of his life as a preacher, to whom we owe many golden words. And the book ends with the statement: "Christianity, however, did not appear." The book was intended as an experiment in thinking through the question, "What would it have been like if Christ had not been condemned and did not die on the cross?"

"There is no Jesus who died for us on the cross." This is the point at which both Jacobsen and Caillois —though with different motives—pick up Paul's question: What if this Christ business isn't true? What if the things that supposedly happened never took place at all? And the chorus of diverse voices answers: "Christianity would not have appeared." If the presupposed events had not taken place, history would have run a

---

* Jens Peter Jacobsen, "The Plague at Bergamo," in *Mogens and Other Stories,* trans. Anna Grabow (New York: Nicholas L. Brown, 1921), p. 101.

different course. And we who would have preached all this, believed it, and based our lives on it would be deceived deceivers, the pathetic victims of a phantom. The irony of the words with which the French writer Unm-el-Banine concludes her autobiography, "I had chosen opium—and Christ raised me from the dead," would become bitterly serious: opium does in fact win the day *if* Christ is not risen, for then the foundations in which the miracle of my own life seems grounded begin to shake.

Thus, although they do so in a variety of often conflicting ways, the writers and poets testify to how crucial it is that the "mighty acts of God" really happened and are not merely symbols of timeless truths. Either God has come to us at Christmas and "the Dayspring from on high hath visited us"—or, like Faust, we grope along, wandering in the dark, barred from a view of the other side. Either Jesus Christ has suffered on the cross for us, and that miracle of substitution has occurred—or we remain chained to the unpurified elements of our life, calling out from a pit in which no one hears us. Either Jesus Christ has breached the front of death— or the boundary of death defines the meaning of our life, delivering us over to the philosophy of "Let us eat and drink, for tomorrow we die" (I Cor. 15:32).

The alternatives become just that stark. The stakes are just that high when the question of truth or illusion is raised about the mighty acts of God. From Jean Paul to Dostoevsky, from Jacobsen to Caillois, authors have seen the gravity of this question of fact more distinctly and with more agonizing clarity than have many theologians. They have seen it even when (like Jacobsen) they were atheists.

But if this is so, then at first blush it seems to be anything but a liberating conclusion! Our faith, if not altogether deluded, has been saddled with some exceedingly taxing problems. One could say it has intruded on a veritable mine field of difficult questions. Does our faith depend on something really having happened, on there having been real acts of God? If so, then it must stand up under the historical question—and the tests of the historian. Then faith cannot simply say, "It's in the Bible," and quietly close its eyes.

For there cannot be two different truths, one that faith believes and another, possibly contradictory, that arises from the results of science. That would lead to the kind of schizophrenia which Lessing once described when he cried out in anguish that his heart was Christian but his head was heathen. If Christ is not also the Lord of our head—our history-minded head—then he will no longer be the Lord of our life either. A Savior who rules only over emotional values and who remains outside the territorial waters of the intellect can hardly lay claim to being called our Redeemer. A faith which ignores or represses intellectual doubt instead of facing it and resolutely passing through it would probably not even be "little faith" (Matt. 8:26). It would be no faith at all.

Therefore it is certainly no sign of piety when I obstinately cling to the letter of Scripture and steer clear of every critical question about the reliability of what is reported there, as if questioning were a sign of unbelief. Anyone who thinks like that does not put much trust in the living Lord. To many such pious folk he surely will not say, "O you good and faithful servant, enter into the joy of your Lord." He will more likely say, "O you of little faith, why are you so fearful? Why do you seek me, the living, among the dead (even among dead letters and words)? Do you think that every little puff of criticism can blow over him whom the wind and waves must obey?" Anyone who chooses Jesus Christ as his total, undivided Lord should not then divide himself into a trusting heart placed at his Lord's disposal, and a critical head which he keeps for himself or—what is even worse—simply puts on ice.

This brings us, then, to the point where we must now ask *how* faith comes to grips with the reliability of the biblical accounts of Jesus. Naturally this is a broad field, and I can only pick out a few central questions.

The first question that confronts faith—as even the rank amateur without historical training knows—arises from the fact that in the original accounts of the evangelists there are many things that do not exactly agree and in some cases even conflict. This disagreement can have various causes, depending on the particular case. One reason, though, is worth mentioning because of its key importance. All four evangelists are not merely reporting events, they are interpreting. Each of them explains the events he records from a quite definite, and highly individual point of view.

Mark's account, for example, as Martin Dibelius once characterized it, is the book of the "secret Epiphany" of Jesus. Mark sees the Son of God living in deep disguise, unknown to his fellow men. Gradually, however, he begins to lift his incognito—the afflicted people whom he helps are the first to recognize him—until finally, on Easter, he discards it completely and appears in his glory. Matthew's Gospel, on the other hand, inserts the drama of Jesus of Nazareth into the total panorama of salvation history. He understands it as the fulfillment of ancient prophecy, and in turn makes it into further prophecy of the future. This is the theme around which Matthew composes his account. Finally, the writings of Luke see the story of Christ as the peak of a line which begins in the Old Covenant and continues through the history of the church to the Day of Judgment. These are only a few bare indications of how the material was seen from varying perspectives and then gathered and edited according to different thematic viewpoints.

An example may make the point even clearer. We all know the story of the great feast, particularly as recounted in Luke. If we examine how this parable is presented in Matthew, it is not easy to recognize the same basic outline. New strokes are added and the accents are differently placed. The prominent man mentioned in Luke becomes in Matthew's version a king who prepares a wedding feast for his son. When the servants—not just one any longer—are sent out, they are killed by those who were invited. The enraged king sends his army and levels the city of those who reacted so ungratefully and brutally to his invitation.

Thus it is that additional features are introduced into the original framework of the parable. The king is a customary image of God, the king's son is a code-term for the Messiah, and the wedding symbolizes the Messianic age of joy and fulfillment. The fate of the king's messengers is an allegory for the blood-offering of the Christian martyrs, and the burned city portrays the catastrophic fate of Jerusalem in A.D. 70.

Thus, in this parable of the Lord, Matthew saw something of the life of Jesus, the struggle of the early church, and also the fate of the Jews. And where he saw these parallels—or where the parable and his historical experience coincided—Matthew blacked in more heavily the corresponding lines of the parable, letting other parts of the picture fade into the background.

Now when I say that Matthew did not simply repeat the original parable word for word but touched it up by commenting upon it and bringing it into a definite thematic framework, am I somehow suggesting that he therefore falsified, slanted, and arbitrarily retouched it? Am I suggesting that this is precisely why the Gospels do not measure up to the exacting standards of modern historiography? For if Matthew had measured up to present standards of correct reporting he would have had to quote verbatim, without any trimmings of his own. Instead of acting like a painter who struggles to interpret the subject of his portrait, he would have had to be a photographer who objectively records what is done and said.

Well, that is precisely what Matthew did *not* do. There is no doubt about it. He did more than give exact testimony. As a witness he put himself into the picture. But how did that come about? Is that simply the primitive way of doing it, whereas we today have discovered refined methods of objective reporting? Or are there perhaps quite different and deeper reasons which, once we have seen them, could immediately strike down our modern pride? *That* is now the question.

This brings us, then, to the second of the central questions we hoped to touch on. The first had to do with the fact that the individual Gospels have different perspectives and center on different themes. Our second question has to do with what this fact implies about the historical reliability of the evangelists. Doesn't everything seem to point to an intermixing of subjective elements, so that their technique of reporting makes it impossible to get back to—as the German historian Leopold von Ranke put it—the events as they really were "in themselves"? Aren't all attempts to reconstruct the figure of the "historical Jesus" therefore doomed to failure? Albert Schweitzer recounted the history of this failure in his book, *The Quest of the Historical Jesus.*

From the standpoint of modern historical writing, it could very well seem that the evangelists had smuggled their own subjectivity and strongly biased purposes into their presentation of Jesus. They undoubtedly did not set out to collect documentation about certain events with the disinterested objectivity of archivists. But why did they not do that? Why do they thus violate our contemporary concepts of historicity?

Perhaps we modern men have a blind spot at this point. We fail to perceive the very simple and basic reason for this behavior of the first witnesses, which is that, for the early Christian church, Jesus of Nazareth was not a figure of the past but the exalted and living Lord whose presence surrounded them on all sides. His words, "Your sins are forgiven," are not part of the minutes of yesterday; they are a contemporary event for those who call upon him today in faith. The chains are broken *now*. One can experience it in his own person and hear them rattle. And where two or three are gathered in his name, he is there among them. He not only *was* Lord, he *is* Lord—and will still be Lord at the last day.

This is the crucial thing to realize. The early Christian witnesses could not help but see the history of the earthly Jesus in the light of his resurrection. They read the story backwards, so to speak.

Although no analogy is perfect, I may help to clarify this procedure by pointing out that we do much the same thing when we depict a historical figure. When we investigate Goethe or Napoleon or even such an abysmal figure as Hitler from a historical standpoint, we clearly begin from the later periods of his life, when his character is most fully developed and has expressed itself most openly in words and deeds. These are the "bright spots"—or, as in Hitler's case, the "dark spots" —of their lives, the key by which the mystery of the person is disclosed and then traced back to his obscure beginnings. It is from here that we ask the questions: What was there in his heritage, his education, or in his whole life's story that made it possible for this or that trait to develop? Where were the seeds for the character developments which we have before us in ripest form?

Thus it is that the evangelists too look back upon the Lord's life from the apex of his development, his presence as the exalted one. Naturally, however, this is the point at which our feeble analogy breaks down. For the presence of the exalted one is something completely different from what we have called, in the cases of Goethe and Napoleon, their ripest development or the "bright spots" in their lives. If Jesus Christ *lives* as the resurrected Lord, if he is our only comfort in life and in death, if all power in heaven and on earth is given to him, and if history with its romantic tales and tragedies, its individual destinies and its nuclear fire, must end before his throne, then when I look upon the historical life of Jesus from this perspective I see it in a completely different way. I view it, as it were, "with new eyes." Indeed, it even gives me a totally new perspective on the whole world. My old standards no longer apply.

How in the world could I then continue to regard the life of the earthly Jesus with the detached interest of an objective archivist? For Jesus is then no longer merely a has-been; he is the one with whom I have to do just now, whose knock at the door of my life I cannot ignore. He is also the one who will not depart from me when I one day depart; my life will still depend on him even in eternity, as he carries me through every judgment. This is what makes even our present world appear in a new light.

And this is why already at his birth the ancient witnesses—and we with them—see heaven open and hear the hallelujah of the heavenly hosts. We stand before the miracle of Christmas night. In the light of his exaltation it becomes clear that this unique individual cannot be explained on the basis of his human heritage alone. It is his origin and his destiny which make him —from the very first—mysteriously close to us and at the same time majestically removed. Practically speechless before the overwhelming power of his presence, the evangelists suddenly come to see in the earthly life of Jesus something unique, something far different from what a mere bookkeeper of history would ever be able to see, no matter how great his attention to detail. They see a lifted incognito, a majesty breaking forth.

When early Christianity thus identifies the lowly Jesus with the risen Christ (Ernst Käsemann), the son of the Nazarene carpenter with the exalted Lord, it is declaring two things. First, this identification indicates that the early believers were simply incapable of depicting the history of Jesus without reference to their faith. How could they shove aside and ignore the really crucial disclosure about him? How could they keep on naively describing the outward incognito of Jesus when they had grasped the secret of his glory, that glory which ikons try to indicate by golden backgrounds and a halo? But this identification of the earthly Jesus and the exalted Christ also declares that the early believers are not willing under any circumstances to let myth replace history. No nebulous heavenly being can stand in for the man from Nazareth. Mythical heights are usually reserved for figures whose outlines fade into the dim and distant past, not persons whose home addresses are known to the people who met them only yesterday.

Early Christianity must be understood as seeing itself in this peculiar position of defending its presentation of the story of Jesus on two fronts. It does not set out with statistical and historical interest to write the biography of an inhabitant of Nazareth; it sees that figure in the light of the third day, the day when the incognito was lifted. At the same time, it does not try to make a myth out of Jesus of Nazareth; it holds fast to the fact that the eternal Word became flesh and "was found in fashion as a man" (Phil. 2:8).

Once faith has been struck by the majesty of Jesus Christ and by his servant form, how could it describe and testify to him in any other way than that which the evangelists employ? How could the believer then remain neutral and aloof? Does not faith spell the end of an objectivity rooted in mere historical interest? Anyone looking at TV films of an earthquake from the comfort of his easy chair would naturally be conscious of the quake in a different way from the man who himself feels the ground shuddering under his feet and sees the sheltering walls of his home suddenly threaten to collapse upon him. But this is really what happens when we face the humbled and exalted Christ. The old world's timbers begin to creak and the heavens open. The veil of the temple is torn in two, the earth shakes, the rocks split, and the graves open. By the way, this description is a direct quotation from Matthew 27, which many of us know as part of Bach's Passion according to St. Matthew; and we hear behind it the master's musical description of the frightened bewilderment, demolishing all objectivity.

Once you grasp what really happened, once you understand what the story is essentially about, and realize that our normal receiving apparatus can't quite pick it up, then much else that would otherwise remain incomprehensible becomes clear. Since the congregation sees the risen Lord also in the earthly Jesus, the words he once spoke become contemporary, as we have already said. But when the historical and the contemporary thus become identified, the contradiction we had sensed earlier in the Gospel accounts is resolved. On the one side there was that "undeniable faithfulness and adherence to the word of Jesus" (Günther Bornkamm) which was pursued with such exactitude by Luke. And on the other side there was that amazing freedom as far as the "historical" wording was concerned. Jesus' word was certainly preserved and passed on faithfully, and yet it was not protected with a bookkeeper's pedantry. In fact, one could very well put it as follows: The tradition does not simply repeat and pass on something he once said; the tradition is rather his word *today*—it *is* his word today.

Finally, one more thing becomes clear. If the reporter is always caught up in the affair himself, if he is not just a neutral spectator in the balcony but is "on stage" so to speak, so personally involved in the drama that it is impossible for him to speak of Jesus without bringing in his own relationship to him, then one can hardly dismiss the "subjective" aspects of his report as the products of a creative imagination. Although many of the words of Jesus which have been handed down to us may not in the strict sense go back directly to the historical Jesus himself but are formulations of the early church—and hence to the archivist not genuine—nevertheless they have not been plucked out of the air and arbitrarily added on. They are rather the church's response to what Jesus has said to her—and means to her. Here, just as in a worship service, the congregation responds simply because it cannot help seeing that it is itself all wrapped up in everything that proceeds from Jesus Christ.

In this drama no one can be merely a spectator, critic, and reporter; one is immediately drawn into the action and forced to participate. No one can simply read back the dialogues of Jesus with the rich young ruler, the Canaanite woman, or Zaccheus the tax collector, as though he were a court stenographer or even a tape recorder merely registering sounds. Instead, by hearing those dialogues of Jesus, I immediately become a participant. I am placed in a situation where everything involves and affects me. The word to the rich young ruler—"sell all that you have"—applies to me. The silence of Jesus toward the Canaanite woman is the same silence under which I too suffer; it puts my faith too to the test. No one can confess Christ without at the same time confessing who and what this Christ is for him, and hence also speaking about himself.

This is the profound and factual reason for the evangelists' inability to report in a simply "historical" sense. This is why they must present their own confession, why they preach and proclaim, why they speak as participants. And when they do this, they do not change, manipulate, or possibly even falsify the original mate-

37

rial; they simply use the only method of discourse which is appropriate to the material with which they are dealing. They use the stylistic method of confession, the statement of those who have themselves been overwhelmed. They cry out with the surprise of those whom Jesus Christ has overtaken in their flight to a far country, whose way he has barred, and whom he has brought home to a peace of which they had never before dreamed.

What an assurance it is that there are interventions and events of such magnitude that they slam the door on any possibility of objectivity. One can only speak of them in stunned amazement, with all the bewilderment of a pardoned prisoner. And how grand it is that there are things which no amount of intellectual inquisitiveness can disclose to us, things that remain hidden from the wise and clever, and are only for those who yield themselves and become involved—as disciples.

As for *who* it is that calls me, this is something I discover only as I follow his call, gird up my loins, and pursue the newly opened path. Only as a disciple do I discover who Jesus Christ is. But then it is only as a disciple that I can also speak! I cannot but testify to his coming, because it is, after all, *my* Lord whom I am going to meet, and for whom I open wide the gate.

3

Understanding
the Miracle
Stories

READING

Jesus made the disciples get aboard the boat and travel on ahead of him across the lake. He intended, in the meantime, to dismiss the numerous people who had gathered around him. When that was done he climbed a mountain, quite alone, in order to pray. As the darkness deepened, he continued there alone. The boat meanwhile, had already gone quite a distance from shore. The waves began to pommel it as it encountered a headwind. However, he came to them in the fourth night watch—over the lake. When the disciples saw him walking on the lake like that, they were shaken and bewildered. They shouted, "It's a ghost. It's a spirit!" and cried out in terror. Jesus spoke to them at once and said, "Don't worry! It's me. Don't be so scared!" Then Peter answered, "Well, Lord, if it's you then tell me to come to you—on the water!" He said, "Fine. Come on." And Peter actually climbed out of the boat, walked on the water, and went toward Jesus. Then he suddenly realized the strength of the wind; fear seized him; he began to sink and called out, "Lord, help!" Immediately Jesus reached out and grabbed him saying, "You weakling in faith, why did you let doubt get the best of you like that?" When they then climbed into the boat, the wind died down. But the men in the boat fell to their knees before him and burst out with, "Surely you are the Son of God!"

Matt. 14:22–23

TEXT

Seeing that a crowd was gathering, Jesus told the disciples to cross the lake. Then a scribe stepped up to him. "Master," he said, "I would like to follow you wherever you go." But Jesus answered, "The foxes have dens and the birds of the air have their nests. But the Son of Man has no place where he lays his head."

Afterward one of his disciples said to him, "Please give me a little time, so that I can bury my father." But Jesus retorted, "Follow me—and let the dead bury their dead."

Then he climbed into the boat with his disciples after him: they followed him. And then a storm, a real earthshaker, broke over the deck. He, however, was napping. So they ran to him, shook him awake, and cried, "Lord, rescue us, we're going down!" But he said, "Why are you so fearful? Why is your faith so weak?" Then he got up and reprimanded the wind and water. A great calm followed. The men, however, were shaken and began to wonder. "What sort of a man is this?" they asked each other. "What can you make of a man who has wind and water at his beck and call?"

Matt. 8:18–27

In the previous chapter we dealt with the question, "How reliable are the biblical accounts of Jesus?" We concluded that the usual standards by which a report's objectivity is measured simply don't apply. The witnesses in this case don't maintain a historical distance from the events they describe but are themselves involved and deeply concerned with those events. They don't report about a "has been" or a "once upon a time." They speak of a Lord who surrounds them with his presence. Through experiences which literally exceed their powers of expression, these witnesses have been given the certainty that this one life did not end in death the way all others do. They are convinced that there is more left here than wistful memories of a great life nobly lived. He is still in their midst. Their hearts burn within them (Luke 24:32), and he remains with them to the end of the world.

Obviously one cannot simply suppress or ignore these later experiences when he looks back and recounts the things that happened during Christ's life on earth. When the evangelists tell what Christ did, what words he spoke, and how he acted in critical situations, they do it literally "in retrospect." They "look back" like people who have had scales drop from their eyes in the meantime and who now know immeasurably more about him than they did when they were "on the spot," noting his words and deeds with dismay and a good bit of misunderstanding. As they see it all pass before them once again, either in memory or in the accounts of eyewitnesses, what might be called the "aha" reaction sets in: "Aha!—*that* was what he meant, then, when he said, 'The Son of Man is come to save that which was lost.' We didn't get it at the time, but now we know that he really does bring the turning point of our life and snatch us out of our lostness." "Aha—*that* was what he meant, then, when he made the blind to see and burst the chains of the bound. He wasn't trying to be a magician who would startle us with every possible miracle in order to make us do what he pleased (what fools we were once to have thought that!). That was his way of letting us know that even the created world is entrusted to him, that he can bring whatever is bungled or derailed back into line, and calm the groaning creation" (Rom. 8:22).

41

Thus they just cannot report what happened once upon a time, long, long ago without constantly commenting upon it out of the store of experience which is *now* at their disposal, which includes their confrontation by their living Lord. Like the ikons of the Eastern church, they now can portray him only in such a way that the newly-discovered golden background comes to light.

For this reason, then, they do not act like archivists who work with historical documents. On the contrary, they are witnesses of a fateful event which has lifted their very life off its hinges. This is why one can never separate the witness from his testimony, nor the testimony from the interpretation he puts on it. The witness always speaks both of himself and of what it is he has encountered. He speaks very personally, but to term this "subjective" is to confuse the issue.

I would like to illustrate all of this by means of a miracle story, specifically, the account of the stilling of the storm. A comparison of the way the three synoptic writers speak of this event will show that, apart from shadings here and there, the basic outlines of the occurrence are all the same. The stories even have the same "slant": He who is so touchingly humble that his homelessness exceeds that of the foxes and birds lets his royal rank flash forth from beneath its concealment once in a while—like a king in disguise whose beggar's robes allow glimpses of the purple beneath them—and here we catch the gleam of him whom the whole universe cannot contain and whose word, therefore, commands the elements of that universe.

Matthew, though, avoids a "photographically" faithful representation. He makes clear his own encounter, and how he comes to grips with what happened and lets that illuminate the account. It is precisely on this individual contribution of Matthew—this "extra" which tells us even more than a mere objective report—that I would like to focus.

The fact that Matthew is not merely objective but in reporting also testifies to something, and in testifying interprets, is not a sign of weakness on his part. It is not as if he were incapable of reproducing a chain of events accurately. His procedure is tied up with the very nature of the subject matter itself. You can't talk about someone who has wind and wave at his command the way you would talk about the weather or report on wind velocity and tides. When you speak about the Lord of the elements, you get into a dimension different from that which deals merely with the elements themselves.

What, then, is peculiar about Matthew's writing? What in this account is his own personal testimony? I want to describe these special touches in a few brief strokes.

First of all, Matthew has placed his account of the stilling of the storm in a different context from that of the other two evangelists. In order for you to catch the significance of this, I must make a somewhat pedantic comment! All experts who deal with the New Testament on a scholarly level agree that the oldest level of the tradition is always to be found at the point of the words and deeds of Jesus, whereas the framework into

43

which these words and deeds are set is a later addition which may be traced back to the Gospel writers themselves. Therefore it is precisely the context in which a saying of Jesus has been placed that can make a writer's intentions particularly clear. At that point he shows you *his* interpretation of the event.

And in fact, this is just what Matthew has done. He has put this account of the stilling of the storm into a unique framework, and thus shed new light on it in terms of the new context. Both the other evangelists string this story on a necklace with Jesus' other miracles. Matthew, however, has put his narrative in the context of discipleship—"following Jesus"—and has then shaped it in the light of this particular theme.

Our passage, of course, is introduced by two stage-setting anecdotes which highlight this question of what it means to entrust one's life to Jesus of Nazareth and to follow him. We first hear of a scribe who, in some way not clear to us, is fascinated by Jesus and offers to be his disciple: "I will follow you wherever you go." Yet he is rebuffed in somewhat the following fashion: "Maybe you are looking for human—all too human —security from me. Has it occurred to you that it is precisely this middle-class security that you could *lose* by following me? You could be turned out in the cold. Through your contact with me you could run into difficulties with the authorities, with the government, with public opinion. In fact, you could even be estranged from your own family and your friends. Do you realize that what you *think* will bring you a good, safe Christian status could actually lead to such crises in your personal life? The foxes have burrows—I don't. The birds have nests—I can't even offer you that much comfort. You have no inkling of the adventures of faith to which I will summon you. So a bit of caution would be very much in place. Better give it a little more thought!"

The second story concerns a disciple who also wants to join Jesus. But first he wants to bury his father—a very understandable and very human reason for digressing briefly from the path of discipleship for a short excursion into personal affairs. He too receives a brusk reprimand ill-suited to the Thorwaldsen-like picture of the beckoning Nazarene which our imaginations tend to create. "Let the dead bury their dead," Jesus replies. "I have called you to the things that make for *life*. I have no use for sentimentality among my followers about the passing age. You must pull up your roots from everything that was your native soil and from which you used to draw strength. Follow me at once, resolutely, and totally—or drop the whole idea."

Then he climbed into the boat "and his disciples followed him." Here we have the key word: they "followed" him into the adventure which Matthew is about to describe. From now on the subject of discipleship is the matter under discussion. The context into which this account is placed thus leads our eye toward this single theme, much like the perspective in a drawing leads our eye to the "vanishing point." Here the central question is what it means, amid the insecurity of raging elements, exposed on the water and cut off from everything that formerly supported our life, to entrust ourselves to this Lord and find a kind of security with him that surpasses our wildest dreams.

Thus it is that Matthew indicates what, for him, is the pivotal point in the account which follows. The indication of that point is Matthew's "contribution"— or better, his confession. It conveys how he, Matthew, reacts to these events on the lake and how he incorporates them into his understanding of faith. By his very reporting of the stilling of the storm he lets us know: "*I* can only see it in connection with everything else I know about Jesus, especially with what has dawned on me since his death. And thus, for me, it is nothing but an exposition and illustration of what it means to entrust yourself to him with all that you have and are, no matter in what 'boundary situation' you may be."

That is the characteristic slant which Matthew gives to his report. Perhaps we can formulate what he confesses by his narration as follows. I have become a disciple of this Lord. Therefore, what I have experienced with him, and what others have told me, I can see only in the light of everything that I have come to know about him. For in following him and in experiencing his presence—his living nearness—today, long after his earthly life is over, something decisive has happened to me. He has transformed my sorrow into the stuff of which a totally new and wonderfully liberating confidence is made. He has given me security in time of trouble and persecution, on the water and in the desert. He has let me know that I am forgiven for all that in my life which I have not brought under control. As I move toward the Last Judgment he gives me assurance that even there he will not desert me. And as I look back on his life, I find that everything I have experienced with him and through him now, shows up in all that he said and did then. It is even woven into the garland of legends about his life. Therefore, I want to show you, my readers, how the point of that life crops up again in this particular story. Here, just as though a picture were being painted before your very eyes, you will see what it means to have this Lord snatch you from the world of death and enable you to live in his peace amid the tumult of the storm.

Our task, then, is to determine how Matthew worked his "discipleship" theme into the account of the stilling of the storm, and how he tied it to his confession of Jesus Christ so tightly that the narrative itself became a confession. Here we can discover the ins and outs of how an evangelist can both write an account and at the same time work it over, interpret it, adapt it, and turn it into a hymn in praise of him who proved himself to be Lord even in that situation, a Lord who revealed his majesty to his astonished companions.

What does "following" mean? That quickly becomes clear in the way that the disciples call out to Jesus when the waves break over the boat and sinking seems unavoidable. Tormented by anxiety now that the end is at hand, and possibly stricken with the misery of seasickness too, they cry out, "Lord, help us, we are perishing!"

This is the first characteristic nuance that differentiates Matthew's account from those of the other evangelists. For in Mark—as in Luke—the cry is quite "secular": "Master (Chief!), don't you care if we are wiped out right here?" That is a totally unedifying, very creaturely cry for help. It is just the way helpless people in a tight spot turn to someone they look up to, expecting that he will know what to do to get them out. Matthew, however, turns this cry into a prayer: they call him "Lord," a title of divine majesty which appears elsewhere in Matthew as a form of address to the coming judge of the world. This is also the word by which the afflicted call out to the man whom they believe has power to loose their chains and free them from their dark bondage. The disciples, too, always address Jesus in this way, once they have been made aware of his hidden majesty. "Lord, help us!"—that is more than a mere cry for help to a stranger or a request for advice from an authority. It is also a confession: "You are beyond the reach of the elements. You are the creator of all things. You cannot be overpowered by things; and these waves are, after all, only things. Therefore help us, we are scared. We see the abyss yawning to swallow us." Thus Matthew put into this prayer-like cry of the disciples what he had experienced in his own life as a follower of Jesus. Jesus had become the Lord of Matthew's life. Matthew had learned to trust himself to his Lord, and he came out of every crisis experience humble about his own power and strengthened in his faith.

The confession of Matthew—this confession in the form of a narrative—comes still more markedly and clearly to the fore, however, at another point. Within the miracle itself, Matthew undertakes to restructure the course of events which had existed in the tradition and been taken over by Mark and Luke. His new rearrangement, which does not alter the facts themselves, is nothing more than a nuance. It is so subtle, so nearly imperceptible, that only the sharp and critical eye of modern scholarship has noticed this virtually microscopic shift.

According to the tradition that Matthew had before him, after the disciples called to him for help Christ rebuked the wind and commanded the raging waves, "Peace! Be still!" (Mark 4:39). And then, in the calm that reigned while the roaring elements still echoed in their ears, the terrified disciples heard him say, "Why are you so fearful? Why don't you have any confidence?"

In Matthew, though, the traditional order of deed and word is reversed. Before the Lord speaks to the elements, he talks to the men. While his companions are still in deadly peril, while the lake boils and the gale rips the sail to shreds—and hence before he speaks his word of command—he talks to them about faith: "You of little faith, why are you such cowards? Have you forgotten who I am? Instead of taking account of the wind velocity and the height of the waves, why don't you count on me? Anyone who looks at the elements instead of looking to me will, in fact, be overpowered by the elements."

And that is exactly what happened. When Peter in a fit of foolhardy faith tried to walk on the water, the fit turned into one of fright. He looked at the water instead of at his Lord—and he sank. Thus, in the crucial moment itself—in the threat of moral illness, in the bomb shelter, in the slowly gathering net of intrigue which others spin for us—it inevitably becomes clear just whom or what we credit with being able to exercise power over us. Is it the cancer, the bombs, the schemers? *Or* is it the Lord of life and death, of body and soul, who thinks his "higher thoughts" about us and leads our human thoughts like waterbrooks?

Some people, though, confront the Lord with the attitude: "First perform a miracle, and then I will have faith in you. First show your credentials, and then I'll get on your bandwagon." Such people will never see the miracle or receive the reward of faith. All those who have experienced God testify in overwhelming unanimity: "We do not believe 'because of' something —'because' it pays, or 'because' we see ironclad proof of God's action so that we know we aren't buying a pig in a poke when we believe." Rather their confessions of faith all strike the common note, "Nevertheless I am continually with thee" (Ps. 73:23)—*even though* we see nothing but the blindly raging elements, *even though* the power of darkness seems to have the last word and man's presumption triumphs. Therefore, it is only in the midst of menacing forces that we can confess and declare who or what God is for us. Here is where it becomes apparent whether we truly believe that even the darkness is only a part of his "higher thoughts," and that one little word from him is enough to exorcise the demons.

By this characteristic modification Matthew thus highlights the theme of faith. And he does so in such a way that this faith cannot be confused with sight. Faith is demanded of the disciples while they still see nothing but foam, spray, and darkness, while they still feel nothing but the overwhelming force of the squall and the smack of the breakers, and hear nothing but the howling gale. For it is in the midst of this witch's cauldron that they hear the word of the Lord, "O you of little faith, you cowards."

Only then, only after he has spoken these words to the men, does Jesus address the elements and rebuke them. And only then does it become "very still." Jesus' miraculous lordship over the elements, therefore, does not produce the faith; it is merely a sort of supplemental demonstration of it. It is the illustration to go with a text which he had already put into words when he scolded his companions for their meager faith and thereby pointed them to himself.

It is just like what happened in the story of the paralytic (Mark 2:1 ff.). There, too, it started with a conversation on faith. Jesus began by saying to the paralytic, "Your sins are forgiven." What was that if not an appeal to faith? He expected, of course, that he would be conceded the authority to make a statement like that, and that he would thus be given a status above all human limitations. And then, once these words had been spoken, once he had called upon them to believe that he had silently broken the chains of sin, he opened the picture book to an illustration by saying to the paralytic, "So that you may know that the Son of Man has power to forgive sins, I say unto you, 'Stand up, take up your bed, and walk.'"

In precisely the same way, Matthew's version of the stilling of the storm could continue, "So that you may 'see' what I previously told you to 'believe' (that I do not come from the depths, and that the powers of the deep therefore cannot swallow me and mine) let the elements be calmed."

Here the extraordinary precision of the statement shows how, in a Gospel, history is written in a way that involves interpretation and confession (and we will want to take a look at the stilling of the storm from this perspective). For in the very way he goes about telling this miracle story Matthew actually does an important job of editing. He reverses the order of miracle and word. First of all, Jesus' companions are confronted by the word—a word that summons them to look in faith to their Lord. As a result, the miracle takes on a new function. It is no longer the cause or source of faith; instead, it has the task of giving additional confirmation to that faith, illustrating it, and bringing it to visible expression. The word which pointed so indirectly and cryptically to his lordship would still have been valid, even if his power over wind and wave had never been demonstrated, even if the disciples, though plagued with anxiety, had found wondrous comfort in the fact that he was with them, and so had brought the sleeping Jesus through the still-raging elements to the opposite shore. This is what Matthew is attempting to say—and he really means to say it!

Thus it is for this reason that Matthew has inserted into the traditional miracle story a revolutionary confession. For while he remains true to the individual features of the traditional account, he has made the miracle itself less important by reversing the positions of miracle and word—the address to the elements and the address to the disciples. His new sequence relegates the miracle to a supporting role. As Matthew tells it, the focus of the story is no longer the miracle, but the word concerning faith and little faith. This makes the whole story both a reproach and an infinite comfort, because it shows how illogical it is to call Jesus "Lord," honor him with a divine title, know he is in the boat, and then at the same time quail before the power of the (only apparently) unleashed elements. The miracle itself, then, is only a sort of echo, a kind of demonstration in the aftermath of the event. The miracle no longer motivates faith but merely makes it more certain. It is a sort of "visual aid" which, in a new and different way, refers faith back to the one to whom faith had already turned. It only underscores the text which faith has already learned to spell out: "What sort of man is this, that even winds and sea obey him?"

Having said that, we arrive at the heart of the problem which we have been circling again and again. We have discovered that Matthew did not reproduce the traditional account with the fidelity of a tape recorder. He reworked it "theologically"; he inserted his own understanding of the miracle and its importance. I now ask: Did he thereby falsify that account? To find the truth must we go back behind Matthew and pick up the trail of the original tradition? This is really the key question if we want to decide how much weight such forms of reporting will bear.

Now obviously we may speak of falsification only if Matthew has brought an arbitrary and subjective element into the text. But has he done that? No, he simply sees in each of the several features of Jesus' life story, as in a microcosm, all that he knows about Jesus Christ, the crucified, risen, and exalted Lord. That is what he has done in the story of the stilling of the storm, too. For the de-emphasizing of the miracle, which he accomplishes in such sublime fashion and with such delicate care for details, is really a general trait recognizable in all the Gospels.

Jesus Christ himself constantly did the same thing. Whenever men demanded signs and wonders he turned them down; he condemned such seeking after signs. Never in his life did he perform a miracle in order to make it easier for men to believe, or in order to replace faith by sight, by something they could see. He knew that a Son of God hanging on a gallows has nothing godlike to sell and doesn't put anything visible at our disposal. Whoever allowed himself to be impressed only by miracles, only by the "show," would certainly have been thrown into confusion by the pitiful figure of Golgotha, if not sooner, for it would be hard to find a more ungodlike sight than that.

And what shall we poor latecomers of the twentieth century do when we read in old books that once there was a man from Nazareth who because of his miracles stirred up a lot of talk and was thought to be both Savior and Son of God? Could that be one bit of help to us? Would we today be at all impressed to read that someone had done such miracles in those days? We could only sigh with Lessing, "It is one thing to experience miracles oneself, and another thing merely to hear that others are supposed to have experienced them."

No, our faith does not live on reports of miracles. We live on the *word* of the Lord. We live on what he himself was, and is, and always will be. We don't believe in the resurrection because we somehow happen to have a miracle story about the events on the third day after his death. We believe rather in the resurrected one who convinces us by all that he says and does, and who thereby makes the miracle of the third day recognizable as an event toward which everything in his life presses. We do not believe in miracles which prove to us that Christ is our Lord; we believe in the Lord himself who performs the miracles, who is able to change our lives, who lets us see all things new, and who is still at hand even today with his miracles, his protection, and his unfathomable guidance.

Matthew did the same thing when he undertook the editing of our miracle story. He added nothing arbitrarily. He merely took the little ray of Jesus' lordship which shines out of this account of the stilling of the storm and put it in relation to the sun itself—to that brilliant sun whose rays are broken into a many-splendored spectrum by the prism of the Gospels. Although the Lord stands also at the center of the original account, Matthew has enlarged him by altering the perspective, so that Jesus looms out of all natural proportions and becomes the key topic, eclipsing even the miracle itself. Thus, Matthew works the total picture of the New Testament—surrealistically if you will

—into this report of a small detail. How could it be otherwise, when it becomes clear that all lines of perspective in the New Testament converge on Jesus Christ himself? The Christmas story, Good Friday and Easter, and finally the return at the last day—all focus on him.

Once we have seen how this narrative technique works—and of course it is much more than merely a literary technique—then its traces become visible in still other parts of our story. Time and again the events in the foreground, which leave an impression on our imagination and are therefore easily narrated, become transparent to a mysterious background, so that the story is packed with symbolical clues. The very expression which Matthew uses for the storm—"the great fury of the sea" as Luther translates it—typifies this relationship. The other evangelists use technical meteorological terms; they give a "weather report." Matthew, however, uses the term *seismos*—from which we get our word seismograph. The term certainly connotes a shaking and attacking of the foundations themselves. As a normal designation for a storm, however, it is quite definitely out of place. The New Testament usually employs this term only in a symbolic sense, to refer to the terrors at the end of the world. The word conveys the idea that the world has come off its hinges, that the demons have been unleashed, that Antichrist has taken over, and that affliction and persecution are coming down upon us.

Matthew certainly chose this many-faceted term "earthquake" for a deliberate purpose. Once again he is not simply narrating, but interpreting through the narrative. We ought to listen for all the overtones of meaning with which the term resounds. What the people experienced on that imperiled boat is a symbol for the perils of discipleship in general. Whenever people get mixed up with Jesus Christ, even the landlubbers among them get a taste of what it felt like in that boat. Nuns in China knew it when they were tortured by the Red Guards. Dietrich Bonhoeffer experienced it on the gallows under the Nazis; and in the course of history a host of martyrs have gone through it. Today too the same drama is being acted out thousands of times in ideological dictatorships.

The apocalyptic earthquake of which Matthew speaks is not the only thing which bursts out of the merely historical features of the account to become a codeword for persecutions and times of need in general. This is true also of a second element: the fact that Jesus Christ was asleep in the boat. Thus, he is with us now in all his power, even when we cannot hear him speak. We have a safe harbor even in the midst of the tempest. Here too he does not meet us on the heavenly level, removed from all earthly suffering, or in a Beyond which knows nothing of our anguish. On the contrary, Jesus Christ is always where we are, where the winds howl and the breakers pour down upon us. He came into the world homeless and had no place where he could lay his head. The homeless and forsaken can know: this man is with me; he walks at my side down the lonesome road and in the forsakenness of the metropolis. He who must die can know: this man too has tasted the pangs of death and will be my brother as I launch out on the deep. He who has suffered shipwreck, drifting helplessly on the sea or on the symbolic sea of life can know (as the castaways in Whittaker's masterful narrative, "It was as though the angels sang") : he sleeps in my boat too, even though it seems abandoned like a nutshell to the play of the elements. He gives me security and enfolds me with his peace, whether by rebuking the elements or by receiving me in a watery grave and escorting me to eternal joy. In fact, that is just what Gorch Fock, a seaman in World War I, wrote in one of his last letters: "If you should receive word that I have been killed in action, do not weep! Remember that even the deepest ocean into which my dying body sinks is only a pool in the hand of my savior."

Thus Matthew is the first to draw the parallel between the boat of the disciples and the ship of the church, which floats along on the sea of this world and yet is protected by the presence of the Lord. Since Matthew's telling of this story and his making it transparent to the majesty of the Lord, this image of the church as a ship has become a symbol which has engraved itself deeply into the consciousness of Christianity. It has comforted, persecuted, and tortured believers in their nights of anguish and forsakenness. Matthew has allowed this golden background to the ikon-picture of Jesus to show through.

Was he, then, a swindler doing a false retouch job, concocting scenes and giving them out to be genuine and historical? Or did he really understand his Lord more fully than all the disciples in the boat who ran to Jesus panic-stricken and crying for help? Which is closer to the truth? As we mature in faith are we not inevitably led to see the majesty of the Lord exactly as Matthew saw it? Are we not thrown wholly upon Him alone, and upon His word?

No one can tell the story of the Lord without at the same time telling the story of his own life, his experience with Him. The Gospel writers have done just that, and that is the key to understanding them.

4

What Are We to Make of the Biblical Expectation of the End of All Things?

READING

Behold, I send you like sheep among wolves, so you must be wise as serpents and innocent as doves. But beware of men! For they will bring you before the judge and wherever you teach faithfully they will mistreat you. You will be hailed before high authorities and even kings for my sake—as a witness to them and to the heathen. When they turn you in like that, don't worry or fret about how or what you are going to tell them. When the time comes you will be given the right words. For you don't have to stand your ground alone, with your own words; the Spirit of your Father is the one who will speak through your words.

The disciple is not superior to his teacher, nor the servant to his master. The disciple must be satisfied with the same standing as his teacher and the servant with sharing the fate of his master. If the master of the house is called "Beelzebub" and "devil," his people will certainly get more of the same!

Matt. 10:16–20, 24, 25

THE BIBLICAL EXPECTATION OF THE END OF ALL THINGS

TEXT

As Jesus left the temple and started off again his disciples came up to him and pointed to the sacred complex of buildings. He reacted by saying, "Do you see all that before you? Believe me, I assure you that there is not a stone there that will stay in its place and not be broken down!"

Then he sat down on the Mount of Olives. And once again his disciples approached him—this time quite alone—with the question, "But tell us, when will all that happen? And by what signs will people know that your return is at hand and that the end of all things is around the corner?" Jesus answered them, "Be on your guard so that no one pulls the wool over your eyes. For a lot of people will come claiming my name and assuring you, 'I am the Christ, I have the answer.' And many will fail to see through such chicanery. Times are coming when you will hear of wars, and not only wars themselves, but also rumors of the threatening danger of war. Keep your eyes open and don't give in to panic! For all that will come, yet the end of all things will not be at hand. People will rise against people, and nation against nation; famine and earthquakes will occur here and there. All that is only the first birth-pangs of the end. Then you will be bullied, and done away with; you will be the prime targets of hate whatever the nation you live in—and all because of my name. Trapped like this, many people will even engage in mutual denunciations and will turn on one another in hatred. When that happens, deceivers with false promises and false panaceas will arise, and many people will be taken in by them. If lawlessness and chaos get the upper hand like that, love will grow cold among the great mass of people. But the man who holds out to the end will be saved. The good news of God's kingdom, though, will be proclaimed over the whole earth as a testimony to all peoples. And then the end will come."

Matt. 24:1–14

In our earlier reflections we came again and again upon the idea that the story of Jesus was not written as a chronology, a mere historical documentary. The New Testament witnesses saw it rather in terms of its end, from the perspective of the exalted Christ who has overcome death.

The same thing is true here where the secret of history itself is being disclosed. It is not done the way a historian or philosopher of history might work out his ideas about the nature of historical processes. Out of the wealth of historical materials they would try to extract general laws of causation and then say, "Look, these are the motivating forces behind human affairs; this is how they interrelate to constitute the course of history." No, the New Testament sees the secret of history in terms of its end, the "death of the world," as it were, from the perspective of him who rises victorious beyond that death.

Perhaps we may risk using an analogy to describe what happens. A drowning man sees his whole life pass before him. Is he not likely to see the several events with even greater accuracy than in the moment when he first experienced them? There is a colorful kaleidoscope of memories: how his mother used to kiss him good-night, how he brought home the first money he earned himself, how he got married, and perhaps how he later spent cold and lonely hours on guard duty in far-off fields of service. It is as though everything that once happened to him by chance and without apparent meaning is now arranged in perfect order, hung up and stretched out like a string of beads, suspended from the anchor point of the end to which it all led.

The passage which constitutes our text points to a somewhat similar process. Almost as by a shock treatment the disciples are suddenly confronted with a vision of the absolute end. As in the dream of a man who is being sucked under for the last time, the film of world history unrolls before them, and everything suddenly makes sense: wars and the horrors of war, earthquakes, terror, and persecution take on new meaning and become signs and signals that point to something. They are the agonies of a world coming to an end; they are the birth-pangs of a new life surpassing human imagination.

It would pay us to think about this last "dream" of those who were drawn into the end. We should reflect on the visions that these words of the Lord waked in them.

It is indeed peculiar how some incidental remark will suddenly cause an ominous certainty to pop into our heads. That happened to me once when I was a little boy. I wanted a truck more than anything in the world. Finally they gave it to me. I thought I would burst with joy. I must have acted quite silly, almost as if I were out of my head. When my father then grabbed it away and carried it into the house, I broke into tears. He took me to task for this sudden outburst and scolded me for my ungratefulness, to which I replied—as he later told me—"It's going to fall apart anyway some day." All of a sudden, in the moment of fulfillment, the evanescence of beauty became clear to me and I experienced the shock of finitude. When Troy was still in full flower, Homer sounded the same note: "The day will come when holy Ilion will fall."

Our text describes a similar situation. People stroll past the temple and then look back from the Mount of Olives to let the solid monumental walls take full effect. They stand as a symbol of durability, a citadel that endures the ravages of time. Ancient proverbs foretold that when the temple fell the world would end. And then Jesus says, "Not a stone will remain on another." He sees bizarre ruins and charred rafters where a copy of the heavenly Jerusalem now rises like a fortress of eternity.

Of course, people already knew that everything is hastening toward oblivion. The leaves fall in autumn, youth fades, and the good old days—they had them then too—give way to a changed world. We too, as we came back to our homes after the war and walked through devastated streets we no longer recognized— we too sensed something of the ultimate oblivion. In the autobiography of Carl Zuckmayer there are the lines he wrote during that war while he was an emigrant on a foreign shore:

> I know I'll see it all again
> and yet find nothing I once left.

This eternal oscillation between becoming and perishing, however, seems to take place against a fixed background: These walls will stand, and the hymns continue to be sung; these prayers will never cease, and the regularity with which the church's "Amen" follows will be a sort of prototype for whatever events are to occur with absolute regularity. If all this too should cease and desist what an abyss would open beneath us!

Secular man too is not immune to such thoughts. He too has the feeling that something will remain, safe from all change. Even if the Chinese take over, the lakes will continue to sparkle, Bach's B Minor Mass will still resound somewhere, and the audacious dome of Michelangelo above St. Peters' will go on being a testament in stone. It would be simply unthinkable that a nuclear war could destroy it all. If that happened, what would be the sense of thoughtful men having sought the truth for thousands of years, of artists having given form to beauty, of people having loved and laughed and searched for happiness? What an abyss, what an absurdity that would be!

Yet, despite its eerieness, the question of the disciples, "When will this (absolute) end come?" is overshadowed by a peculiar peace. They tie the question about the fall of the temple and of the world to the question of the Lord's return. Thus, the triumph of God stands at the end of all endings. And therefore, the dissolution of everything that exists or counts in the world is not totally without a note of comfort.

Of course, that is also true elsewhere. Our greatest anxieties do not stem from the intensity of our pain. They arise when we cannot see any point or sense to the pain. Job had probably endured bodily and spiritual attacks much more severe than those we read about. What finally threw him was not the pain itself, but the abyss of emptiness that opened before him. Weren't the deaths of his children, the disastrous fire, and the loathsome sores that befouled his body a monstrous contradiction of everything he had formerly held to and believed? Didn't this completely nonsensical punishment of a righteous man refute any divine governance of the world, any "higher thoughts"? Wasn't it all so terribly senseless that there was no point in living any longer? Didn't this make a mockery out of all holy writ and truths of faith? Hadn't the holy phrase "I am the Lord your God" been replaced by the cynical conclusion "You never know. . . ."?

That was Job's suffering! It was not simply a matter of physical pain. Think for a moment of what it would mean if everything that the folk singers and recording artists sing about—love, death, parting, longing, fulfillment—were simply wiped out without a trace! What if the silence of an absolute end would spread like a godforsaken desert across an earth that was once the home of Plato, Lao-tze, Albrecht Dürer, and Beethoven? Then the abyss of total meaninglessness would open before us also. This is probably the seat of that secret fear which is kindled deep within us at the thought of the world's atomic self-destruction. The fact that you and I could be killed in such a holocaust is surely not sufficient to explain this fear. After all, we can't be deader than dead, and we could be just as dead from falling off a ladder or being hit by a car. No, the fearfulness lies in the snuffing out of everything that exists or matters and of every meaningful principle and truth for which anyone has ever lived.

The disciples, however, can no longer be carried away by this ultimate fear, since it is the Lord himself who uses the destruction of the temple as a symbol for the total end of the world. They know that someone is standing beyond the end who will receive them when they emerge from the fires of that destruction. They know that someone is there beside them always, even to the end of the world, and that he awaits them on the other side of the great abyss.

For them this is far more than a mere forecast of the distant future. Mere hints of the future leave us just as cold as mere reports of a past when God supposedly performed miracles and was on friendly terms with Moses and other figures of ancient times. How distant "once-upon-a-time" is! And how distant the future is! That's why it leaves us cold. Therefore it is not the mere prophecy of the end that bothers us here and now. If the astronomers tell us that our earth will meet its death by fire or ice in a few million years that doesn't spoil the taste of our steak one bit. Intellectually it may be very interesting, but existentially it is irrelevant. It doesn't affect my life in the least. My loves, my hates, and my scale of values remain untouched.

The whole situation changes radically, however, as soon as Jesus tells us that *he* is the one whose work is being carried out in the tumults of the end, and that he will come again in a new and apocalyptic repetition of Christmas. News like that changes the present too. Such a future reshapes the now. It becomes so decisive for the present moment that many contemporary theologians, taking proper note of it, allow themselves to be led astray. Stressing the present relevance, they conclude that the message doesn't really refer to the Lord's future and his impending return at all, but is merely a cryptic, futuristically phrased statement about the present. The future tense is supposed to be a disguised way of saying that every moment of our lives is the end of the line, lived as a "moment before God."

No matter how mistaken this conclusion may be, one thing is sure. If the Lord is coming again, if all the floods and fires that cleanse the world will subside before his throne, if at the Last Day those who have been saved need not look back into a world-wide grave wherein lie buried—according to the famous vision of Jean Paul*—also their ideas of God and their dreams of a heavenly Father, if instead they are able to sing, "God has brought us to this place"—I say, if all that is so, then the present moment of my life is also radically changed. Then my death is not merely a departure, but a going home. Then war and terror, plane crashes and mine disasters, marital difficulties and stays in the hospital are no longer simply impersonal results of natural processes; they cease to be "visitations" and become "visits." Someone is there. His heart is both the source and the goal of it all.

That is not to say that we understand the plan of God. How often it remains obscure and puzzling to us! We humans often see no difference between God's plan and a sphinxlike fate. Yet, we trust him who makes the plan. We trust him because we know Jesus Christ.

No one has expressed this transformation of the moment and its terror more profoundly than Christ himself as quoted in John's Gospel (John 16:20–21):

* See p. 12, n. *.

". . . you will weep and lament. . . . you will be sorrowful, but your sorrow will turn into joy. When a woman is in travail she has sorrow, because her hour has come; but when she is delivered of the child, she no longer remembers the anguish, for joy that a child is born into the world."

In the same way we look at life differently when the Son of Man comes again and is once more "brought into the world"—this time openly and in majesty. Then our pains become birth-pangs. They are the very opposite of those toothaches and turned ankles which make me ask in irritation or despair, "Why did this have to happen to me, of all people?" To be sure, birth-pangs lead to that difficult time when "her hour is come," but they are filled with joy and anticipation of the great event ahead. And so, even the "hour" is lived under the brightness of Advent. This is why images of motherhood always stand at the crucial points of salvation history. There is the Virgin Mary in the stable of Bethlehem at the first coming of the Lord, and there is the woman in travail (Rev. 12:1–2)—the symbol for believing mankind—whose pain and sorrow are mysteriously transformed and hallowed because they press toward a great fulfillment: The Lord is about to come. The hand of the clock moves a little closer to twelve.

I cannot rest on this greatly comforting certainty as though it were a pillow, however. It is not a secure possession, but must be won anew every day. It must be achieved through the "nevertheless" of faith. The Lord depicts what terrors lie ahead in order to show that one does not possess this certainty with the black-

and-white assurance of a mathematical rule, but must snatch it again and again from the fire of doubt and temptation. These terrors are already in the offing. They rise up in consecutive waves even as the earth quakes before the destruction of the temple. In Nero's time entire cities in southern Italy and Asia Minor are reduced to ashes and rubble. Imperial coups bring war, bloodshed, and political upheavals. In Caesarea there is a Syrian-Jewish conflict that results in the massacre of thousands of Jews. And yet all this is only a sample of history as a whole with its ever-recurring destruction and terror. World history, in fact, is a dreadful parallel to the cruelty of nature. Nations eat and are eaten. The sequence repeats itself with the rhythm of all natural processes. In earlier days people feared the Huns, then it was the Turks, then the French, then the Germans. Today people fear the Communists or Black Power or the Yellow Peril. It's always the same. However, that is not to say that faith remains untouched by this struggle and that believers have a metaphysical inside track that lets them slip through or nonchalantly stand above it. That certainly is not the intention of Erich Kästner's phrase, "The believer knows more."

No, says the Lord, when unrighteousness gets the upper hand, the love of many will grow cold. No wonder it turns out that way! People can get by for a while with the idea that God directs the woes of history toward his great fulfillment. Then when the going gets tough, luck runs out, and burdens hang heavy upon us, we can still comfort ourselves by saying that God is purifying us in this fire and preparing us for better things. Only, he'd better not pile it on too thick! For there are two instances where this sort of comfort breaks down.

First, when the pain becomes too great, when a person is suffering the torments of hell—perhaps in the agony of a heart attack—he is so racked with pain that he can no longer ask about its meaning, to say nothing of growing in maturity because of it. He cries only for relief, for a tiny pause to catch his breath.

The second case in which complications arise occurs when the pain lasts too long and just won't let up. I can take it for a year or two. I can tell myself, "God is permitting you to pass through this school of suffering." I even realize that I needed something of the sort— "needed," for now I have gotten beyond that stage, I have mellowed and have come to my senses, I have learned my lesson. After this, any further torment would be absurd. Nevertheless, the pain continues. In this case Erich Kästner's phrase, "The believer knows more," becomes out-and-out irony. Faith has to face the fact that a man is not only run through the wringer, but stuck between the rollers. This is the point at which I encounter meaninglessness. At least I am not able to discern any meaning. And for me, meaninglessness invariably becomes a refutation of God.

Returning to the Book of Job, we can spot exactly that breaking-point beyond which even-tempered trust turns into cold confrontation with the void. In the first stages, when Job still imagined himself to be in the school of suffering, he thought he could find meaning, and so he said with pious resignation, "The Lord

71

gave, and the Lord has taken away; blessed be the name of the Lord." But then, when he thought he had graduated from the school of suffering and there was nothing more to learn, yet the torment not only continued but broke over him with greater fury, Job gets mad at God.

So love can in fact "grow cold," as Jesus said, when unrighteousness gains the upper hand and I see nothing but demons on the loose, when the "fat bellies"* and proud spirits hold the field, when their baseless claim that "Might makes right" seems to be confirmed, and their sneering question "Where is your God now?" meets with no rebuttal from heaven. Then it is that faith—which is the theme posed by our Lord in this chapter—comes to crisis. Because he is hidden from us, our faith is stretched to the limit. We live only on the hope for which he has given us his word, the hope he has sealed with his life and death. This hope is that one day faith will be able to see what it has believed —and that unfaith will have to see what it has not believed!

In the Old Testament God made known his name: Yahweh, which means "I am who I will be; I will be who I am." To plumb the depths of this expression is to reach the ultimate appeal to faith, for God does not use it to make public some plan for world history, nor does it reveal a cosmic strategy. It lets us know that we are like children walking into the dark by a path that leads through rough spots and chasms, through "the Land of Unlikeness" where we will "see

---

* *Fetten Wänste* is Luther's term in Psalm 73:7.

rare beasts and have unique adventures" (Auden).
But at the same time the promise holds that through
all the insecurities, he remains steadfast, and that when
we have nothing else we will learn what it is to have
him. For he will remain "the same." If our love grows
cold, he will still burn with love toward us. If we
break with him, he holds on to us. "He is who he
will be."

For this reason we know that one day he will be
all in all and that what our faith now sees only in a
mirror and gropes after as if in a smoke screen will one
day stand clearly before us—that is, Jesus Christ will
come again. It has not yet appeared what we shall be.
But then it will appear. Thus our faith pushes us and
pulls us toward the future. We stand before doors that
have yet to open.

How absurd, then, is the question whether one can
still be a Christian, whether the old Book still has
something to say. The people of the Bible are not
backward-looking people. Far from it. They are oriented more toward the future, toward what is coming.
They have put their hand to the plow and gaze toward
a horizon where darkness is ending and the first red
of morning gleams. The key word is not a reactionary,
backward-looking "still," but a simple "already": the
devil has already fallen like lightning from heaven; the
kingdom is already in your midst, where Jesus Christ
is. Therefore, despite terror, persecution, and catas-
trophe, the cry is not, "Watch out! Take cover!" but
rather the vibrant message, "Lift up your heads, for
your redemption draws near." The darker it gets, the

nearer the day, and the closer God is to you with his surprises. What the godless see as a confirmation of the "death of God," filling the night of their lives with yet deeper darkness, becomes for you a confirmation that the Lord is near, that he is coming to meet you from the other side.

The text also hints at a background to all we have said, a final secret of history: Although God permits terrible things to occur as warnings to us about the world of death, in a remarkable way we humans ignore those signals and cover the chasms with glittering nets of make-believe. The Lord says that "Christs" will come, pseudo saviors, promisers of salvation, visionaries. For even ideological dictatorships cannot rule by terror alone. Hitler himself said that. Terror must disguise itself, otherwise it would be too frightening and would create its own opposition. Therefore it must call on compelling ideas as camouflage. It must promise the opposite of what it really is. It must say "freedom" where it means enslavement; it must speak of "protecting the world" when it pursues imperialistic goals; it must praise "humane ideals" when it is merely interested in the usefulness of manpower for the production line; it must speak of making people "happy" when it robs life of all magic and lets a drab greyness settle over everything.

Others may derive comfort from misleading visions, but for Christians, such ideas lead to persecution and loneliness. "They will deliver you up to councils," says the Lord. The system of legal rights, which really is only a system to promote the interests of the rulers, will take all your rights away. You will be outlaws, like sheep in the midst of a wolf pack. But when you are abandoned like that, you will also be given signs whereby you may know that you are secretly removed from this doomed historical process and are being borne along by the Lord of history himself. Instead of you defending Christianity, you are the ones who are being defended. "What you are to say will be given to you." The battle-line runs between Christ and Antichrist. It is not you in all your weakness who must hold the front. The gauntlet has been thrown down to God himself and it is he who has accepted the challenge. He makes your cause his own. He takes over the defense; you have his backing in court. Here again amid the storms of history, the words of the Lord speak to us, "O you of little faith, why are you so fearful? Am I not with you in the boat?"

But what does all this have to do with us? Is it not like pouring water on a duck's back? After all, we live in a nation based on law with a relatively stable constitution, and with Christianity built solidly into our national life. If anything, we have almost *too* cozy a place and *too* many special privileges. What do those apocalyptic horrors which prefigure the end of history have to do with us? Aside from indications of occasional economic crises and the flaring up of certain social problems, we live quite comfortably. Even the world-wide "balance of terror" doesn't bother us too much. These feelings, however, by which we keep the Bible's powerful visions of the end at arm's length are deceptive and even a little provincial. We must recognize that this peaceful calm and relatively orderly situation is only a brief pause, a tiny moment in the total sweep of history. Spatially too it applies to only small portions of the globe. The situation can be quite different just a few hours away from our hometown.

The Bible, however, always has the whole in view, while we men see only what is right under our noses. That's what makes us truly provincial. Sometimes we think the Bible is removed from reality when it speaks about things that don't specifically knock us over the head. But the Bible simply encompasses a broader experience of reality than we do. It knows of the dark potentialities which lie dormant in our world, just waiting to surface, because it sees the heart of man revealed in the light of eternity. In that light we learn that the events of Auschwitz did not happen by chance; they represent a possibility latent within all of us, slumbering there. We also learn that sleeping dogs can be roused when the hour of darkness arrives. With brutal realism Dostoevsky once said that a hangman is hidden in every man; and Adalbert Stifter speaks of the tiger-like disposition in each of us which is quite tame in the normal everyday situation, but which even a bad case of nerves can prod into murderous and destructive passions. Actually what the Bible means by the death-agony of history is none other than the long-suppressed evil potential of the world which is pressing toward a final and visible outburst.

"But he who endures to the end will be saved." What is this end, and how does one achieve such endurance? The nature of the end and the method of the Lord's return elude our imagination. In the Old Testament the coming lordship of God is sometimes described in earthly images which by their fantasy—"The wolf shall dwell with the lamb" (Isa. 11:6) —merely make us aware of how the Incomparable exceeds any earthly comparison. In the New Testament these attempts to fit the coming kingdom of God into the framework of our perceptions cease entirely. Nowhere does the kingdom appear as a utopian vision or as a reign of peace at the end of history. On the contrary, these human dreams are demolished; they become the unpaid debts of false Christs and empty-handed demagogues. Just as the resurrection account gives no hints about the physical structure of his glorified body (I Cor. 15:39–50), so there are no statements about the "how" of the Lord's return and of the coming kingdom. The announcement that he will come on the clouds of heaven is certainly no statement of latitude and longitude; it is simply a way of indicating the public nature of his appearing. We have only his word—his non-pictorial word if you will—that he is coming again. And our faith says "Amen" to that because it knows that the Lord in whom it believes is not just a figure of our own imagination; he is really in control, both East and West lie peacefully in his hands. And these hands will be all that is left when East and West have become ruined reminders of the mortality of our world. As the world perishes by flood and fire a rainbow will once again shine over it. That too is only an image, suggested again in the last book of the Bible (Rev. 4:3; 10:1) But above and beyond all images we reach out for him whom we already possess as Savior and whom we know will be with us always, even to the end of the world.

But how do we "endure" in this hope when the times of testing come and everything seems to speak against there being a God? What do we do when the mournful news gets around that God is dead, and that we are "by ourselves" on that desert which Nietzsche, Jacobsen, and even Sartre describe as the now-godless wasteland of our life.

We certainly will not make it through by stubbornness and by conservative clinging to our "Christian heritage." Jesus says that instead we are to watch and wait for him—for him who comes over the waves to meet us from the other side.

But isn't that an obscure way of putting it? What does it mean to speak of "waiting on the Lord"?

I wait for an important letter, hoping it will finally come in the morning's mail. I wait for the results of a medical examination. I wait for the outcome of events in Vietnam. I wait for the definitive break in the cold war. I wait for that date tonight. But how about the Lord whose coming I cannot visualize? Does this waiting for him, this enduring to the end, have any real place in my life? How is it done?

Yes, this waiting *does* have a place in my life. I certainly do not do it by looking out the window to see whether there is any sign of the Son of Man, whether flames have sprung up on the horizon. Those who wait for the Lord to come must lay claim to him where he presently is. Whoever does that, however, discovers that this presence of the Lord today has about it a forward-looking aspect that points beyond itself toward fulfillments yet to come.

But what is this presence of the Lord? How do I have him with me today?

I have him in my neighbor. This neighbor is hungry and asks if we have something to give him (Matt. 25:35); he is an exile and asks if we will take him in; he is sick and asks if we will visit him; he is imprisoned and asks if we will come to him. And in all of this the Lord himself is there—he who at the same time is at the end where there are no more prisoners, no sorrow or weeping, and even death is no more; where the tears of every eye will be wiped away. We have him here in our neighbor. And it is because we have him and hold him here that we can also "endure to the end." We can never be flat on our backs, without any hope at all.

Why, then, do we get discouraged? Well, it's not because we are lacking in devotion or don't think about him enough, or need more practice in the art of waiting. A good part of our discouragement stems from our constant preoccupation with ourselves. We take ourselves so awfully seriously. And when we do that, everything in life goes haywire. Our worries blow themselves up into immense bugaboos; our little self-conceits play a disproportionate role, and if they are disappointed they never stop gnawing at us. "We build castles in the air and drift further from our goal." Most of our miseries arise, not because we find ourselves in an objectively miserable situation, but because we define both misery and joy in a false way—with reference to ourselves. Most of our neuroses too derive from this same self-centered-ness.

In his fine book *Behind the Forest* Gerhard Nebel tells of a nurse who is wrapped up in her work, knowing nothing of the joy of playboys and playgirls and not looking for it either. But in the poverty of her simple life she is brimful of joy, passing it on to the patients in her care. Then he says the only effective means of combating neuroses and depression is self-sacrifice, not the game rooms at Las Vegas, or pampered lap dogs, or cocktail parties—only self-sacrifice will do. For it is the Lord whom we meet in our neighbor. When we hold him here, then he holds us. When we serve here, then our loins are girt and our lamps burning. Those who call upon his presence here learn to know his inexhaustible riches—and to await still more. The longer they believe, the more insatiable is their hope; the greater the fulfillments they anticipate, the less importance they put upon themselves. It is this shifting relationship between small and great, important and unimportant, which must thus be properly arranged if it is not to produce neuroses and perplexities in my life.

Jesus Christ reveals these last things to his followers, for he can scan the horizon of history from beginning to end. He sees the twilight of the day, the twilight of life, and the twilight of the world. And in the all-consuming desire of his love he says, "Would that even today you knew the things that make for peace!" We, however, do not hear him. We are too wrapped up in our daily work, our life's work, and the world's work.

At the beginning of the war I stood in the bell tower of St. Katharine's Church in Danzig with the church organist. He sat down at the keyboard of the carillon to play a hymn on the hour. His mighty proclamation of the gospel rang out over the whole town. The bells beat upon my ears and the sound of their message so filled me that no other sound could intervene. Far below, though, I could see men going on about their business. They were building an air-raid shelter. The excavator clattered, pneumatic drills hammered away, and traffic surged along. No one looked up to listen to the music that was pounding in my ears and filling me to the brim. What sounded all around us up above remained inaudible down there below amidst the noise of man's daily work.

Have we heard the sound that comes from above? We certainly cannot stop our machines. Nor should we try. But we can pay attention to the sound that filters through our earthly noise. For the air is full of promises, and we would lose everything if we failed to hear them.

A
Look
into the "Lab"

Postscript for Theological Readers

The four sermons in this book were first preached in St. Michael's Church, Hamburg, at monthly intervals during the winter of 1966–67. For over twelve years I have been preaching series of sermons there in the same church, each of them organized around a specific theme. This Hamburg congregation is the most varied imaginable. A goodly number of the worshipers are always visitors who otherwise have little or nothing to do with the church. During this particular series the large attendance of young people was also particularly noticeable. In this postscript I should like to share with my theologically trained readers some of the considerations regarding principles and methods which guided me in my preparation.

As far as basic principles are concerned, I began with the idea that the present theological discussion between the "modern"and "conservative" camps—the labels, by

the way, are not only inadequate but downright misleading—ought to be treated from the pulpit. It speaks
very badly for the relation between classroom and pulpit when newsmagazines and popular intellectual jour-
nals can give the impression that they are letting the
public in on what the theologians are hatching in their
ivory towers and discussing in their esoteric circles, or
when "back-to-the-gospel" movements can—and perhaps must—arise. The fact is that as preachers we have
all been saying too little, on the fatal assumption that
anything we said would be "expecting too much of the
congregation" or would stick in their craw. It is somewhat paradoxical that in a time which has made the
concept of a "world come of age" into a theological
slogan, the congregation is considered unable to con-
sume anything but a milk which has been previously
run through the "edification" separator and laced with
the additive of "harmlessness." If, on the other hand,
a preacher has not thought through the problems which
historical-critical biblical research and basic hermeneutical scholarship pose for us—if he has not mastered
them theologically—he may indeed have good grounds
for assuming that it would be "expecting too much of
the congregation" for him to dish out that undigested
mishmash from the pulpit and label it the "bread of
life." In that case, however, it is not the immaturity of
the congregation that is the roadblock but the fact that
the preacher himself has not yet mastered the problems theologically.

Different generations of preachers face these difficulties in different forms and in differing degrees. When

it comes to the problems of what people like to call modern theology, older men frequently feel themselves too uncertain to say anything solid. It is possible that their method of skirting the issue or ignoring it altogether shows more character than righteously indignant public condemnation of books one has never read. Younger men, however, are still wrestling with the questions, and their impatience with their uninformed —and hence often very self-assured and legalistic— congregations tempts them to speak in ways that are disturbing and upsetting for their people. This might be a fruitful tactic for a master of the socratic method, but in inexperienced hands it can easily sound impudent and destructive, thus solidifying the lines of opposition.

For myself, I thought it necessary to speak openly to the congregation, and other interested people, about these live issues—especially about the key question of the relationship between faith and history. The sermon topics themselves indicate the problems which were uppermost in my mind.

My treatment of these problems differs from other possible approaches in that I preached on them within the context of a worship service. I would consider it a misunderstanding of my method if someone should think that I did this for the sake of popularizing the problems. Naturally in addressing such a large and varied group one must try to speak so that everyone understands. One must keep in mind the assortment of viewpoints, categories, and questions which obtain in an assembly of this sort. Nevertheless, popularization was not my primary concern. On the contrary, I am convinced* that preaching has primacy over theology, and that theology merely works back to investigate the basis of that which it has already heard proclaimed. It seems to me to be a perversion when contemporary theology is regarded—especially by many of the more avid young disciples of the masters—as an undertaking which first must investigate the possibility of preaching and lay down the conditions for it. This false primacy of theology seems to me to be one of the decisive reasons for the current spiritual and homiletical paralysis of which we are all aware. The fact is that the primary decisions are reached in the preaching, where the active Word becomes Event. Here is where the great theological themes begin to take shape. They are not first posited by theology in the form of a priori constructions.

Naturally, to put it thus is an oversimplification, for there is no such thing as "pure" proclamation. Preaching is always permeated with theological reflection. The third sermon shows how this was true already in the Gospel accounts. What I mean by the primacy of preaching is not so much a question of chronological priority. It is simply a matter of whether the decisive accent falls on proclamation or on theology.

By the same token I know of no theologians, even among the most modern, who explicitly state that the task of theology is to undertake the formulation of such a priori constructions. But in some covert fashion

* I have given my reasons in a brief essay entitled *Die Angst des heutigen Theologiestudenten vor dem geistlichen Amt* (Mohr: Tübingen, 1967).

it always seems to come out that way, especially among the younger Bultmannites who, not being as deeply rooted in the biblical texts as their teacher, get bogged down in hermeneutical studies and endless prolegomena instead.

To me it is the subject matter itself which seems to demand the proclamatory form of statement. At the same time we cannot hide the fact that the one who proclaims it is himself a theologian, and that he cannot step out of his own skin when he enters the pulpit. He will naturally bring his theological briefcase with him, even if he doesn't dangle it visibly in front of the congregation. But it is precisely when he has arrived at a theoretical position on these questions, and can even place them appropriately within a more comprehensive dogmatic framework, that he should beware lest he forget the critical criterion of every theology: it must be preachable, because its very origin is in preaching.

We become so very much involved with the problems in historical-critical biblical study, problems in form criticism, problems in the relationship between faith and history, and the methodological questions of hermeneutics. But since these problems are all of a theological nature, they too must be preached. They too must become a part of the proclamation. What I have attempted in the present series is simply to demonstrate this fact. It was my hope that the congregation would be more open to these questions once it sees that they can be stated sermonically and that the hymns and prayers of the service do not act upon them like antibodies—or vice versa.

In terms of method, the hardest problems for me were the following, and I mention them only because it may be worthwhile for others who wish to tackle this most urgent job. First, it was crucial to find appropriate texts to serve as models for presenting the questions. This was not an easy problem to solve, and perhaps it was not always solved happily.

Then too, the questions themselves could only be treated from a few typical angles. For example, the account of the stilling of the storm seems to me to be especially helpful in showing that there is never an instant of pure preaching or of pure historical writing, but that the specifically theological pattern—the "interpretation by the witnesses"—shapes the account from the very first. I am deeply indebted to the work of my friend Günther Bornkamm for valuable suggestions on this matter of the history of tradition, as those who know the literature will already have noticed. For the problem area of future and present eschatology treated in the fourth sermon, the commission of Jesus to his disciples seemed to me to be a fruitful starting point. Here it was often a particularly complicated business to fix the dimension of faith in which certainty about the future could emerge. I hope that the background of my theological readers will help them recognize in this connection much which I could only hint at in the sermon itself. Indeed, I was happy to find that the very question I had hoped to elicit from my theologically oriented hearers was in fact raised after the third sermon: In principle, are we modern preachers so very different from Matthew when he views the traditional miracle story in the light of the *total* manifestation of Jesus Christ, the resurrected and exalted one?

Methodological mastery of the task also required a copious use of the art of omission. Anyone who has the slightest idea of the subtle variations, the ramifications, and the sheer immensity of the questions I have raised will sympathize with me in the hard job of choosing all that is to be left unsaid. The specialist, if he is at all sympathetic, will notice at once that some difficulties have not been omitted altogether but simply dealt with in an oblique fashion. The fact that something was left unsaid need not always indicate that the preacher was unaware of it. Four sermons allow no more than a sampling of the subjects. And even a sermon is limited in length. These four are no exception, though the fact that they were preached on Saturday afternoons enabled me to tax the patience of my hearers to a greater than normal extent.

Perhaps I may be forgiven, then, if I simply make reference to a few of my previous works in which at various points I have given what is essentially the theological background for these four sermons. I would mention first *Theological Ethics 1: Foundations* (Philadelphia: Fortress, 1966) and the suceeding volumes for which English translations are now in preparation. It is curious that theologians in the field of ethics still tend to overlook the question of the shift in our modern understanding of reality, leaving it instead to the hermeneutical investigations of the New Testament exegetes. Either that or—as in Harvey Cox's brilliantly written *The Secular City*—they attack the question with no regard for method or for casualties along the way. My thesis is that theological ethics must be understood as a Christian interpretation of reality, and that the modern shift in the understanding of reality suggests the importance of a fresh interpretation of the world in the light of law and gospel. In the *Theological Ethics* one might note especially my treatment of such questions as authentic and inauthentic accommodation in telling the truth, and the new understanding of the orders, war, property, marriage, etc. I might make mention too of two other books in which I have treated the present themes somewhat more fully: *Between Heaven and Earth* (New York: Harper, 1965), pp. 1 ff., 14 ff., and 39 ff.; and *The Trouble with the Church* (New York: Harper, 1965), pp. 11 ff., 22 ff., and 65 ff.

The present book is of course only a first attempt to bring up to the pulpit firing line the questions normally discussed far back at theological "headquarters." I am aware of that, and I know too how risky and imperfect this attempt is. It has had the merit, however, of making some people stop and think a bit.

I am a little worried about one possible reaction from the theologians who read this book. They might think I am trying to mediate between positions as a kind of mediating theologian. This impression could certainly arise from a superficial reading, since I try to take seriously both parties to the current debate. My purpose, though, is simply to make each aware of the other, and to bring critical viewpoints to bear on both. Other than that I have no desire to wage direct warfare against any particular school. It is remarkable, isn't it, that the lines have become so firmly fixed that people think everyone is bound to take one side or the other—as if there were no such thing as a third position totally different from the other two, a position which arises not through synthesizing or mediating but simply through asking the questions differently.

Most theological thought today runs on strangely inflexible tracks. There are only two or three main lines, usually identifiable by the names of individual theologians. I don't know whether these rail lines have reached their limit yet. There is much to indicate that in the meantime—at least at "headquarters"—other routes are being projected and new ways found. Despite popular opinion, the familiar established routes are no longer the only ones available. I have offered these few bibliographical suggestions in order to indicate that my reason for not belonging to one or another of the present schools is not traceable to mere fence-straddling or the desire to mediate. It lies rather in my endeavor to think the problems through for myself and to stake out fresh terrain.

Type, 11 on 13 and 9 on 10 Baskerville
Display, Optima and News Gothic